"We have known Beverly for more than 25 years and have been amazed at her strength and her faith and trust in God through much trauma during those years. Many times she was alone in her darkest hours and yet she never faltered in her faith. She speaks with authority and confidence as she shares from deep experiences, and much success as well. She is a great mom and grandmother and a wonderful, loyal friend to so many around the world. You will be blessed by her story and inspired by the principles she lives by." —Jim Janz, global entrepreneur and mentor, Canada

"Every intelligent businessperson wants his or her business to prosper. It is fulfilling when an enterprise flourishes! The Bible paints a vivid picture of a prosperity that extends beyond sole enterprises, partnerships, and corporations through all of life and into eternity. I call it whole-life prosperity. Bev calls it wholeness. Wholeness pictures a financial soundness and abundance that transcends the narrow bandwidth 'prosperity' rooted in the American Dream. No one wants to hit a home run at work and strike out at home, or be forced out in relationships.

"Bev's fresh insights and transparent account of her own journey toward whole-life prosperity in *Sunday Morning: A Step by Step Journey to Wholeness* will make you laugh, maybe tear up. Bev doesn't just talk the talk, she walks the walk. She's audio-visual. What you see matches what she says. So open your eyes, open your ears, open your mind. You'll love this." —Ken Johnson, Pastor Emeritus, Westside Church, Beverly's home church, Oregon, USA

The Rest of Their Quotes!

Sunday Morning tells the "rest of the story" behind Beverly Sallee Ophoff's amazing business success. And on the next two pages, you'll find the "rest of the quote" excerpts that appear on the back cover of this book!

This approach to telling *more* can be taken as a metaphor for the life message Beverly offers in this book! Some things in her life and speaking have been purely "business"—but always, the truth undergirding her business principles has grown out of the *faith* journey that has shaped the totality of her life. The women quoted below are an example that there is always more than can be said about a person's character and faith.

From Australia

"This book is a rare privilege to enter into the innermost thoughts and experiences of one of the most loved and successful business women in her industry.

"There are abundant personal and leadership lessons to learn from this transparent, humble, beautifully written account of Bev's life journey, exposing the adventures, personal encounters and disappointments, joys and the wisdom gained through lessons hard learned.

"Using her unique musical and communication abilities to inspire thousands globally to rise up to claim their financial freedom—her story tells of the most important freedom of all, knowing and loving Jesus as her personal Saviour.

"Her examples of courage through faith, guidance through prayer; her heart and understanding of the deep needs of people and how she has helped so many—inspires us to become all we can be. There is real guidance here of how we can individually claim our own personal joy and freedom through faith." —*Glenda*

From Sweden

"Beverly Sallee is one of the finest leaders in our industry. Her ability to lift people to higher levels of belief and performance is legendary.

"*Sunday Morning* is a great book by one of the wisest women I know. This is a book I will return to and read over and over again.

"Thank you, Bev, for sharing your journey on your way to wholeness." —*Christina*

From South Africa

"Beverly touches on some fundamental human values and principles that hold true for ALL religions and cultures. She reminds us that the universal principles of TRUST in the Higher Being, FAITH, GRATITUDE, HOPE, FORGIVENESS, and PRAYER are resounding truths throughout all humankind.

"Worldly matters belong in our hands, but God Almighty belongs in our hearts! Life is intended to be centered in Oneness of purpose, Worship, and the Love for God. If one directs their sight toward this, everything else will fall into place." —*Farah*

From the USA

"Beverly sprinkles the truths of the gospel around the world. She brings all of her values and beliefs to thousands of relationships in every continent!" —*Kathy*

From India

"What a wonderful book from a woman, who is as dynamic in business as she is in ministry, with a heart for God and for people! Beverly transparently shares the secret of her leadership—taking God as her team leader and her counselor. The chapter on her personal journey is tremendously moving. Having known Beverly personally for a number of years, we can confidently say that the principles she shares about forgiveness and having a heart for others are exemplified in her own life. If you want to discover the source of her joy, I highly recommend you read this book ... and then read it again!" —*Suzan*

Sunday Morning

A Step by Step Journey to Wholeness

Beverly Sallee Ophoff

Bible quotations are drawn from a number of sources, primarily:
THE NEW KING JAMES VERSION (Thomas Nelson Publishers,
Nashville, 1983)

Other versions and translations cited include:

New American Standard (NASB)

New Living Translation (NLT)

The poem, "I Stand By the Door," on page 136, is used with the
permission of HarperCollins Publishers.

Comments about this book may be sent to Beverly Ophoff c/o Premiere
Training Concepts, at 2660 N.E. Highway 20, Suite 610, PMB 28,
Bend, OR 97701.

ISBN: 978-0-9760881-1-0

Cover design by Diane Peterson, petersondesign@cox.net
Interior graphic set-up by Starr Clay, starrclay@comcast.net
Photos by Larry Crossman, Arthur Ophoff, studio404photography.com,
and Tamara Wytsma

Foreword

As I write this, I am sitting on the lanai at a condo in Kauai. I have been coming here for more than thirty years. Each annual visit serves as a "marker" in my life, and a time for evaluating how far I have come and how far I still have to go! This trip, my husband Arthur and I are celebrating five years of marriage. How blessed these years have been! I have discovered that when you wait for the King to show you *His* plan, He makes all the difference!

My prayer is that in sharing my journey to wholeness, you will find encouragement and hope along *your* way to Him. He is the ONLY way to live.

Dedication

To my grandchildren: Skylar, Karsten, Cayden, and Harper Aspen! I cherish the memories of my grandmother's faith. I trust you will find strength in my faith and love for you.

I also dedicate this to all those who need to forgive and be forgiven. I learned by difficult experience to forgive everyone, *so I could be free.* Romans 3:23 tells us, "For all have sinned and come short of the glory of God."

I acknowledge with deep gratitude those who helped me back to the Lord by their compassion, love, and forgiveness.

First and always: Heavenly King Jesus, my Savior and Deliverer.

Earthly king Arthur, whose unconditional love for me helped me finally to grasp how much God loved me.

Jim and Nancy, dear friends who loved me and invited me to join them on a new path that made all the difference.

Debi and her husband Mark, and Paul and his wife Jessi, my precious children who loved and forgave me through it all.

Fred and Florence, who constantly loved, listened, prayed, and encouraged me.

Jim and Sharon J., who kept me sane in the darkest hours.

My only sister, Barbara, who lives in heaven with our King. She was always there for me.

Jerry and Karen, precious friends, who introduced me to Arthur.

Dr. David Beighley, friend and counselor.

Bill and Camilla, warriors who prayed and encouraged me and my children always.

Rolf and Erika, priceless warriors from Germany who led me to healing and restoration. Thank you, Ingrid, for introducing me to them.

Helmuth and Martina, my music friends from Germany who invited me into their world of performance in many nations. They were lifelines through it all. Sara and Rahel, their daughters, I claim as my own. Now I enjoy their sons-in-law: Carsten (Sara) and David (Rahel), and their grandson Joseph.

Roberta Hromas, who showed me a future in His Kingdom by introducing me to Israel and sharing her love for it. The trip with her to the "heavenly land" was unforgettable.

The praying sisters: Glenda, Sue, Nancy, Renee, Kathy, Jeanette, and many others who, through various means, told me they were praying. I am so grateful. Please *keep* praying!

The late Dr. Charles Farah, professor at Oral Roberts University, who prayed for me to receive the baptism of the Holy Spirit and taught me the deeper things of the Lord.

Dr. Jan Dargatz, my chronicler, encourager, and friend for life.

Thanks also to my friends who were willing to contribute their experiences and testimonies to this book: Jules, Jan, Tera, Daisy, Ingrid, Laurie, Diane K., Florence, Kathy, Maria, Martina, Clarissa, Sharon L., Bev F., Arti, Else, Diane O., Pat D., Sharon J., Dina, Alicia, Farah, Renee, Michelle, and others I am sure I will recall later. You know who you are and how you have helped me through the years.

Contents

1

The Sunday Morning Meeting

A hurricane was brewing off the east coast of Australia, and we later learned that we were the only plane allowed to take off that day. The flight was extremely turbulent. I arrived late for the first venue of three weekend speaking events that called for me to be in Brisbane, Sydney, and the Gold Coast. Australia is a big place! Look at a map and you'll see that these three locations are a *long* way apart. There was nothing on my schedule except speak, fly, speak, fly, speak, and fly—nothing *between* speaking and flying!

Even given the weather and the long hours of travel, I *knew* I was supposed to be in each place and felt privileged that I had been invited to speak, especially at the weekend's "spiritual service," where I could speak freely about my faith.

In many places around the world where I have spoken to business-related audiences, my time to speak was on Saturday night. I was honored to fill that premier time slot. But I also began to ask various event planners, "Do you think we could ever have a service or a meeting time on Sunday morning?" Initially, there was little interest in such a meeting. But, over the years, the event planners began to schedule a service time on Sunday morning, which was otherwise an "off-conference time slot." This meant that the speaker did not need to limit what was said to information related to the business plan we were presenting and encouraging others to pursue.

While this time on Sunday morning was rarely called a "worship" or "religious" service, the planners knew and the speakers knew, that what was shared on Sunday morning was related to a speaker's beliefs and values, and was not limited to business principles or opportunities.

I never have felt that I should mix Saturday night and Sunday morning. On Saturday night, I shared what I know works in building a business, and specifically, what worked for me in building my businesses. On Sunday mornings, I shared what I know to work in building a person's spiritual life—and more specifically, what worked in building *my* spiritual life. I feel very free to share spiritual principles and truths on Sunday morning. In many ways, this book is "Sunday morning." My other books are focused on BUSINESS. This book is focused on the reasons WHY I have pursued building the biggest and best quality business I can.

On this particular trip in Australia, the planners of the event told me later that at the end of my talk, nearly two thousand of the three thousand people who came to the Sunday morning meeting raised their hands to accept Jesus into their lives when that invitation was given at the end of my talk. These people then went into a side room to meet with people to receive additional information about how to continue walking in their newfound faith.

It was a difficult day, in the natural. And one of the most challenging trips I have ever experienced.

In the spiritual realm, it was one of the most humbling and encouraging and meaningful days and trips of my entire life!

A good business pursued diligently and with the right training tools can change a person's life—and in that, change their family life and even the life of their extended family, neighborhood, or nation. A spiritual decision can change a person's eternal destiny—and in that, there is great joy!

Values Transcend All of Life

I recently published a new book about doing business: *A Woman's Guide to Bootstrapping a Business*. The book is decidedly a *business* book. I do not believe, however, that anything I have written in that book is contrary in core values from what I am writing in this book. This is not a book about spiritual values as such.

This is a life-testimony book. It is different in nature and in scope. My concern here is that a person gain something that is ETERNALLY beneficial to the whole of their life. Thus, this is a book about spiritual values.

Please be assured—I do not live a "divided life." I infuse every day and every appointment with the *whole* of me. I bring all of my values and beliefs to every business event or meeting.

I recognize, however, that we all tend to set aside times for *specific* goals and tasks. Most people who have jobs have certain "work hours"— even if they are self-employed or retired—as well as certain "family or at-home" hours. Those set times are usually fairly predictable. People who work out regularly or who are learning new skills often have "practice hours" in a day, or on certain days. Everybody has "awake hours" and "asleep hours." We set meetings and appointments that are certain time lengths.

My point is this: You are WHO you are as you go into each segment of time that you have designated in your day. A life of genuine integrity is a life in which you display and function in the same set of beliefs, values, faith, and overall "identity" no matter where you are, what time of day it might be, or the group or individual you may be with.

I discovered through the years that whether I was speaking to a very large audience or meeting with home groups or counseling people one on one, people were *watching* my life as much as they were listening to my words.

They were looking to see how I applied my values and beliefs to my work and business. They always seemed to be looking for the "inside Beverly," not just my outer presentation. I came to know that it is only when we begin to know a person's inner motivations and character that we truly can begin to trust another person. And trust is integral to business success, as well as personal success.

My primary goal, of course, is not to gain the trust of a *person*, as much as to encourage a person to put their trust in God. I certainly want others to feel they can trust me, and I take their trust in me very seriously, but in the end, it is far more important to me that they begin to trust their Creator. If there is a goal for this book, *that* is the goal— learning to trust God in a way that is value-based, faith-infused, and character-building.

In many areas overseas, it was years before I was allowed to host or be the main speaker for a Sunday morning service. The first such service I had, I played the piano and sang as part of my business presentation on Saturday night, and at one point in my playing and singing, I stopped and spoke just this one line, "If you want to know more about that, I'll be sharing tomorrow morning on that very truth." I had no idea what to expect. There were about ten thousand people in the audience on that Saturday night, but nobody—not the event planners and certainly not me—knew how many of the people who heard what I said would show up the following morning. Nevertheless they rented a hall near to the main conference center where our meetings were held. And the next morning, I arrived to find people filling all the chairs, sitting on the floor in the aisles, and standing along the edges of the room. My dear friends Gad and Melissa spoke, and I sang and spoke, and we had a wonderful time of sharing the Lord with the people gathered there.

After the service, a Chinese woman came to me and said, "Beverly, you must tell me how I can know Jesus."

I asked her, "Do you have a Bible?"

She said, "Yes."

I asked, "Are you reading it?"

She said, "I am trying, but I am having a hard time understanding what I read. I'm in a part of the Bible called Leviticus...."

Oh dear. Most English-speaking Christians have a hard time with the book of Leviticus! I said, "Go to the book of John," and I showed her where that book was in the Bible. I had the privilege of praying with her to accept the Lord into her life. That time of prayer was worth the entire trip to South Africa as far as I was concerned.

Four Lessons I Learned

I learned four very important lessons as I began to speak on Sunday mornings.

First, *if* a business presentation allows for opinions, the factual content of a business plan can become riddled with all *sorts* of extraneous ideas, including those that might be related to politics, social commentary, and a wide variety of soap-box opinions related to personal likes and dislikes. I certainly wouldn't want to go to a business meeting and be subjected to a long speech from someone trying to get me to believe in a philosophy or religion that is not at all what I believe, or even care to consider. I have respected the general decision to keep business and spiritual agendas separate.

Second, I have learned in life that God has every person on a unique timetable for hearing about Him and coming to know Him. I believe every person on earth has an opportunity, at some point in their life, to say, "God, I need You." It may be a very small window of opportunity, with a very limited view. But the Bible tells us that if we take even the smallest step toward God, He covers the remaining distance to us. We might only take a four-inch tentative step, but He spans light years of time and space to get to *us*. He finds a way to meet the sincere desire of the human heart that wants a relationship with Him. I would never want to violate a person's genuine freedom of choice when it comes to making a God decision, and I have trusted God to bring *His* choice of people to the Sunday morning meetings.

Third, I learned to accept whatever opportunity was given to me to share my personal faith, regardless of venue, time of day, or the amount of time allotted to me. In general, the Sunday morning meetings were extra meetings on a conference schedule. Sunday morning was considered free time, and the business conference participants could choose to attend the Sunday morning meeting or not attend. The venue was nearly always a smaller auditorium apart from the main conference arena where our business-related sessions were held. Nothing about the Sunday morning session was obligatory or mandatory for business participation. Great! Opportunity was provided, and I ran with that. I valued the opportunity given to me, and I valued the free will and free choice given to others!

Fourth, I learned that I must never become discouraged by the "results" of a Sunday morning meeting. Early on, I trusted that God had prompted those people in attendance to be there to hear what He had put into my heart and mind to say. I knew I had to do my part, and do it as well as I could. But the consequences, or results, were up to Him! God is the One who brings a person into a full reconciliation with Himself. He saves the lost soul, and satisfies the hunger of the human heart. I considered the remnant of the larger audience to be *God's chosen people* for the message that was going to be given that day, in that hour.

Taken as a whole, these four lessons learned put me in a position to trust God completely with the messages that I gave on Sunday mornings, and to trust God to enable me to speak with as much vulnerability and transparency as I could. Speaking about matters of faith is very *personal*, and the more I was willing to be "personal" with an audience, the MORE God seemed to use what I said for *His purposes*.

I don't know where you are on God's timetable for your life, but because you are reading this book, I am going to "see" you in my mind as a person who is attending a Sunday morning meeting. I value your presence in this audience. I am trusting God to share *through me* a message that will resonate in your heart and mind—not just today, but ultimately, for all eternity. I pray He will warm your heart, and shine His light on the truth He has for you.

2

The Essence of My Message

I f I could only give you a thirty-second Sunday morning message, it would be this:

> I know with great certainty that God has a plan and purpose
> for your life. He is *not* through with you. He has a
> tremendous future awaiting you. Trust Him to *continue*
> *to create your life* and to bring you to wholeness
> and to give you the tremendous gift of eternal life.

To get the full essence of my Sunday morning talk … read on! I truly believe this chapter is for you, regardless of where you are in your faith journey. If you are devoted to a religion other than Christianity, I offer this chapter to you as insight into a Christian's worldview and beliefs.

If you are breathing, and if you are reading this book or are listening to someone who is reading it to you … then you can be assured that God has allowed you to live to precisely this moment so you can hear His words of love, mercy, and forgiveness. He has a plan and a purpose for your life. That is the Bible promise in Jeremiah 29:11, which says, "I know the thoughts that I think toward you, says the LORD, thoughts of peace and not of evil, to give you a future and a hope." In one translation, this verse says that God's thoughts are always for our *welfare*. God's concept of *welfare* is that you "fare well" in every aspect of your life!

Jesus' repeated words to those He healed and delivered during His earthly ministry were these: "Be made *whole*."

God has a total-life purpose for you, and He not only is *capable* of helping you and healing you, but also *desires* to do so.

The precise ways in which God works in our lives is not something that we get to define, nor can we put our own timetable on God. God's methods are very often beyond our knowing. The prophet Isaiah gave these words of the Lord:

> "My thoughts are not your thoughts,
> Nor are your ways My ways," says the LORD.
> "For as the heavens are higher than the earth,
> So are My ways higher than your ways,
> And My thoughts than your thoughts.
> For as the rain comes down, and the snow from heaven,
> And do not return there,
> But water the earth,
> And make it bring forth and bud,
> That it may give seed to the sower,
> And bread to the eater,
> So shall My word be that goes forth from My mouth.
> It shall not return to Me void,
> But it shall accomplish what I please,
> And it shall prosper in the thing for which I sent it."
> (Isaiah 55:8–11)

Let me point out three key ideas in this passage:

1. You are never going to fully understand what God has planned, what He is doing, or how He is going to use what you say and do down through the months and years ahead. We can *trust* God, however. And, we can feel peace knowing that God is *always* going to know more about everything than we know.
2. God does all things with PURPOSE, and His purposes are for good.
3. God is always in control and what He says He is going to do will be what He does.

The New Testament also gives us this encouragement: Jesus Christ "is able to do exceedingly abundantly above all that we ask or think." The glory WILL belong to Him and to Him alone. (See Ephesians 3:20–21.)

The good news for YOU is that God *is* at work on your behalf, and what God purposes for your eternal good *will* come to pass.

I read the passage above from Isaiah often, to remind myself—especially on busy, chaotic days that sometimes seem unproductive or just frustrating—that I have a purpose that is much deeper than any external circumstance or outward experience. *You* have an *abiding* purpose, too!

While wholeness is at the heart of the Bible's message, and is the end goal of faith, the related truth is that *nobody* is whole *yet*. Every person is on a quest for wholeness.

Every Person Has a Need. I once heard a famous evangelist say, "Every person is sick in some way." At the time I first heard this, I and my children were in excellent health and I momentarily dismissed the fullness of what this preacher was saying. But the more I thought about this statement and the more experience I gained in life, the more I came to agreement.

Sick is a word we usually associate with a disease or ailment. But it also can include a number of other physical difficulties—weakness, disability or inability, injury, and so forth. Furthermore, there are all sorts of "sicknesses." There is a sickness of the mind—both the sickness of the psyche and the sickness of the brain.

There is a "sickness" that can develop in relationships. Any relationship that is not in keeping with God's commandments is ultimately a "sick" relationship. There is a sickness produced by poverty—it is more than simply a lack of material or natural substance (and having insufficient food, clean water, energy resources, and safe shelter). Prevailing deep poverty nearly always produces a prevailing low self-esteem or sense of "no value"—both individually and collectively.

At the core of every person is the possibility of "spiritual sickness." Many people refer to this as sin—either as a prevailing state of the person's soul, or the bondage of guilt and shame that is often experienced.

I have no intention of getting bogged down in a philosophical discussion here. Rather, my presenting the concept of sickness is aimed at these applications:

- Recognize that every person you encounter in any given day is a person who has a degree of sickness in his or her life—he or she has a need.
- Need is often perceived as a "lack" or as a "void" of some kind. Some people are experiencing a full-blown "bout of trouble." The need is obvious and measurable. Other people have a need that is a nagging feeling that something is missing or that something just isn't quite right.
- The process of MEETING or filling a need is an act of healing, in the broadest sense of the word. It is the application of a particular technique, substance, or concept that answers a question, solves a problem, or provides the "missing element." The tools of healing are numerous, too many to ever recount here. Healing can be instituted by a prescription for medicine, a surgical procedure, a counseling session, confession and repentance, a job or employment opportunity, and on and on the list might go.
- At the foundation of all techniques associated with healing is this: LOVING, which is a form of GIVING.

A quest for wholeness is a major part of any "faith journey."

The Role of Faith

Just as faith is rooted in the nature of a loving God, there is a force in the world that is *unloving*. Jesus, and the Bible as a whole, presents this unloving force as the *devil*. He is called a liar, and the father of all who lie, are deceptive, or engage in evil. Jesus said he comes into every person's life with an attempt to steal, kill, and destroy. (See John 10:10.)

All problems and extreme needs that we face *function* as a temptation of the devil to get us to turn our back on God, rebel against Him, or abandon our walk of faith. The devil is the source of all lies and all evil, and God makes it very clear in His Word that He does not tempt people or entice them to sin. Neither does He send calamity our way in order to trip us up in our walk of faith. (See James 1:13.) The Bible clearly teaches that no problem—especially no temptation—is beyond a Christian person's ability to withstand it in faith. The apostle Paul wrote to the early Christian church, "No temptation has overtaken you except such as is common to man; but God is faithful, who will not allow you to be tempted beyond what you are able, but with the temptation will also make the way of escape, that you may be able to bear it." (1 Corinthians 10:13)

These are amazing words from a man who experienced as much tragedy as a person can experience—at least in my opinion. The Bible tells us that he experienced "forty stripes minus one" on five occasions, was beaten with rods three times, was stoned and left for dead, was shipwrecked, spending a night and day in deep waters, and in his journeys he often faced the perils of robbers, accusations by his own countrymen, persecution from Gentiles, and threats from false brethren. He knew weariness, toil, sleeplessness, hunger, thirst, cold and nakedness, insufficient nourishment, and an abiding sense of "burden" for the people he was leading to the Lord. (See 2 Corinthians 11:22–33.) If Paul could experience all this and not be overcome to the point of giving up his faith, surely it is possible to withstand any persecution that might come our way!

Does all sickness and tragedy have some sort of "temptation" at its origin? Very likely so. A person may not personally have experienced temptation and yielded to it, but somebody did, somewhere, at some time in that person's past—or in the course of human history.

Even if temptation is not at the core of a bad situation, the way *out* of any negative situation—as Paul says, "the way of escape"—is directly related to our faith or to the prayers of someone who has faith in praying on our behalf.

We Are Not Wise to See Ourselves as "Victims." Even though we are tempted and attacked by the enemy of our soul, we are never authorized by God to see ourselves as a "victim."

In the later chapters of this book, I share very candidly some of the difficult experiences of my life, but I want to be quick to share with you that I do not feel myself to be a "victim" in any way, and I do not believe in the least that my difficulties have been unusual or more devastating than the difficulties of countless other people around the world.

The Bible tells us that there is sufficient trouble in any given *day* to keep a person focused on the negative aspects of life. (See Matthew 6:34.)

I choose to focus on the *positive*. This does not mean that I live in denial or choose to stay ignorant when it comes to the works of evil on this earth. I know and believe that the devil is continually on the prowl, roaring like a lion to instill fear in people and seeking those he might devour (fully capture in a way that renders his prey incapable of anything other than silence about God or outright rebellion against God). (See 1 Peter 5:8.) Victims are often people who believe they have been targeted in a special way for tragedy. Well … they may have been targeted … but so is *every other person.*

The truth is, the devil is after *every* body. He doesn't target only the poor, obscure, or struggling, and neither does he target only the rich, famous, or successful. He targets the *unsuspecting* and *unaware.* He tries to pick off the easy prey, just as a lion facing a herd of wildebeests. He goes for those who are marginalized, weak in faith, and meandering through life without clear faith or purpose. His temptations are always being broadcast, and no person is ever totally immune from temptation—not even the person you think of as incredibly strong in faith or very successful in ministry.

Temptations come, and we cannot avoid them. But, as one person once said, "We can keep the temptation from nesting in our mind." For example, you can't avoid seeing the lewd or sin-enticing images on a billboard that is forty feet long and twenty feet high and placed strategically on the street down which your taxicab is traveling. But you can refuse to dwell on that image, seek to recall it later, or develop a fantasy about whatever was being suggested.

How do we resist temptation?

The Bible gives a very clear two-part approach. First, we are to submit to God—in other words, know God's commands and intentionally set our will so that we intentionally *choose* to obey them. We are to draw close to God in our prayer and devotion. And second, we are then to resist the devil—simply saying, "I will pay no attention to you. You have no part in my life or future. In the name of Jesus, leave." The Bible says that when we do these things, the devil *will* flee. (See James 4:7.) The devil may return, but in the immediate moment, he must GO.

It is always a great help to quote the Bible to the devil out loud in the time of temptation. That's what Jesus did when He was tempted by the devil during a forty-day wilderness experience. (See Matthew 4:1–11.) We need to know the Word of God, of course, and memorize portions of it in order to be ready to use it as a "sword" in our spiritual battle against the devil. (See Ephesians 6:10–20, where spiritual warfare is described, and the Word of God is referred to as a sword in verse 17.) I regret with all my heart I didn't know the power of this weapon against the enemy. Don't give way to fear and self-pity as I did. You will lose your way.

The Opposite of Faith Is Fear. Many people seem to think that the opposite of faith is doubt, but the Bible repeatedly has illustrations and teachings that tell us the opposite of faith is FEAR.

Fear is very often what causes us to become paralyzed to the point that we can easily become depressed or fall into despair. Fear often frustrates us to the point that we become confused and disoriented, and are increasingly less productive or effective. Fear is what makes temptations so appealing—we see substances and various activities as giving us a way out from feeling pain, rejection, loneliness, or the brunt of persecution.

We must recognize fully that FAITH is ultimately the force that enables us to overcome fear and tragedy. Faith is *believing*. It is believing two very specific things: 1) God exists. 2) God is a rewarder—in other words, God is good and His great desire is to give *good* things to those who serve Him. The Bible says this very clearly: "He who comes to God must believe that He is, and that He is a rewarder of those who diligently seek Him." (Hebrews 11:6)

According to Romans 12:3, *every* person has been given a measure of faith, and God desires that we use the faith we have been given to *believe* for Him to act on our behalf, and ultimately, to turn all things for our good. Romans 8:28 is a favorite verse for many Christians, including me: "We know that all things work together for good to those who love God, to those who are the called according to His purpose."

All things means ALL things—nothing is too dark, too catastrophic, too devastating, or too painful to be left out of God's promises. God can change any situation, turn the heart of any persecutor, and create newness out of decay. He is omnipotent—all powerful at all times over all things. Never, never, NEVER discount God's ability to change what seems to be unchangeable.

The Role of Loving and Giving

Every act of love, service, and positive encouragement is an act of giving. Giving meets needs. It heals.

People in the business world often speak about a "bottom line." They are referring to a financial conclusion that is either positive or negative—a business is either making money or losing money. On occasion, the bottom line is zero—things are at a standstill or all inflow has been matched equally with all outflow (income, expenses; gain or loss; input and output). The concept of a bottom line is not limited to money and business, of course. There is a bottom line to most of life's ebb and flow.

I have been in some of the poorest areas of the world. I know what extreme poverty looks like and smells like. I know that extremely poor areas have way too little input of what is good, and way too much influence from evil in all its forms.

I also know that the purpose of a business is to make money. If a venture is not geared toward making a profit, that doesn't negate its value. That venture might be a charitable not-for-profit enterprise. It might be a good deed or a fun club of some kind. But for something to be called a business, it must be geared toward generating a profit.

And in my thinking, profit is a good word. The more cash flowing through a business, the better. That does not mean that I favor exorbitant profit-making that gouges workers or creates inequity or unjust social situations. Without money, however, there is no reward for workers, no expansion of business, and no opportunities to generate projects that can help the general good of a community, city, or nation!

Everywhere I have been involved in creating new business opportunities, I have also taught those to whom I am extending opportunity, *Find a way to give!* Come up with something that you truly see as a problem, and come up with a solution to which you can devote a part of your thinking, your time, and the contribution of your resources.

Businesses are not the only entities that "make money." People need to make money to live—and that is true even for those who make a "living" by working a benevolent welfare system. We are to be good managers of our money so we might have a "profit" at the end of the day—our income should exceed our expenses so we have something to GIVE to extend the Gospel to those who haven't heard it, to bless those who are facing material need beyond their current earning ability, and to promote growth and development anywhere we can!

The best purpose for being in business is to generate the funds to be an ambassador of good to this very "sick" and need-filled world in which we live. It takes money to fund new hospitals, build new schools and orphanages, give loans to people willing to work to support themselves, and to build churches and Bible schools and clinics. It takes money to give scholarships to worthy students in every endeavor of study. It takes money to create things of beauty that can inspire others to greater accomplishments and quality.

The purest, undiluted giving is LOVE. That is the motivation behind all forms of giving. It is the "renewable" energy that allows a person to give and to continue to give even without a desired result or any reciprocity.

Jesus taught that when we give anything—including acts of LOVE—we are in a prime position to *receive* from God. Jesus said, "Give, and it shall be given to you, pressed down, shaken together, and running over." (Luke 6:38)

To know that we are initiating a cycle that *will* result in our receiving gives us a legitimate reason to HOPE!

Hope is inevitably linked to the future, and to one's self-identity. Hopeful people see themselves as being *worthy* of something better in life. I have encountered tens of thousands of people around the world who had almost *nothing* in life *except hope.* It was the spark of hope in them that led them to jump and even clamor to say "yes, please" when they were given an opportunity for a better life. As much as I have promoted a business plan around the world, I know I have been a purveyor of HOPE.

In many ways, hope is what leads a person to seek and then pursue, and then develop OPPORTUNITY.

The good news about hope is that, like love, it is a renewable resource. It can be rekindled, re-energized, renewed, restored, and refocused.

The Role of Persevering

Jesus taught, "He who endures to the end will be saved." (See Matthew 10:22.) Jesus was speaking about people who were persecuted—hated and reviled by other people. I believe the teaching also addresses those who are persecuted by life's circumstances. The last book of the Bible, the book of Revelation, has laudatory words to say about those who "overcome" all tricks of the devil and persevere in following Christ.

Another way of looking at this is: Those who set themselves to enduring, *no matter what* and *no matter how long*, are going to be those who experience the full rescue that God is already in the process of engineering and bringing about. God is not ignorant of your situation. He is already at work on the solution!

The New Testament book of James tells us that we should regard every difficult experience as a challenge in our life that will help us emerge wiser and stronger. James 1:2–4 tells us: "My brethren, count it all joy when you fall into various trials, knowing that the testing of your faith produces patience. But let patience have its perfect work, that you may be perfect and complete, lacking nothing."

There are some learning processes that are slow—and they cannot be hurried if they are to be effective and lasting. We must seek to LEARN all we can from any situation in life, and especially from negative situations.

In *everything*, there is something to be learned about what works and what doesn't work, what produces good fruit and what produces bad fruit, what is in keeping with a person's talents and dreams, and what is beyond the person's innate giftings and desires.

In *everything*, there is something to be learned about the nature of God, the nature of other people, and one's own human nature.

In *everything* there is something to be learned about setting priorities, making deliberate and wise choices, working efficiently, doing everything to the best of one's ability, producing goods and services known for quality, recognizing the impact of "right timing" and/or "proper sequencing," and understanding the value of goal-setting.

In *everything* there is a kernel of God's eternal reward and a seed that can produce earthly blessing.

In *everything*, there is an opportunity to grow mentally, emotionally, in health and substance, and in the spiritual gifts bestowed by God.

In *everything* there is an opportunity to show love, give witness to Christ Jesus, and experience more of the presence and power of God flowing in us and through us to others.

Yes …

Faith.

Love.

Perseverance.

All three are vital to a spiritual quest for wholeness. But we should be encouraged—we do not do these things *alone*.

Your Five Teams

I believe every person is dealing with the "teams" in their life, in priority order without variation.

First, you must deal with yourself. You are a team of one! You must get your own values and priorities in line before you attempt to lead anybody else. When you settle your faith in God then He becomes number one.

Second, if you are married, you are a team with your spouse. You will not be effective *fully* until you are both on the same page with regard to your values and business.

Third, if you have children, you are a team as a "family." Your children must have an understanding about *why* you are doing what you do, and their place and role in all that you accomplish.

Fourth, you are a team with your sponsor—the one who brought you into your business or who has worked with you as a mentor or partner in the establishment of your business.

Fifth, you are a team with those you supervise.

Too many people go into business or into a new job and they only have concern for their employees. They wake up months, perhaps years in the future, and discover that they have lost their children, their spouse, their mentors, and most importantly, their own sense of identity, direction, and purpose. You *must* keep the teams in your life *in priority order* … all the time, with consistency. That's the only way to stay strong over time, and to have an ongoing sense of fulfillment and meaning. Trust me—your "employees" or those who work under you in some type of organizational hierarchy—will not suffer if you give priority to your own identity, your spouse and children, or meetings with your mentors. THEY will benefit from the good relationships you have with those who are above them, and in the end, they will admire you for your priorities.

You Are Not Alone. You may think today that you are entirely alone in your tragedy—or that no other person has ever been through what you are experiencing. The Bible says otherwise. There is somebody right now who knows exactly what you are going through, and very likely, someone within only a few miles of you who is going through something you would consider to be worse than your situation.

We do well when we seek out other believers who can join with us in prayer and faith as we go through a struggle of any kind. We do well when we seek out support groups of people who are experiencing a difficulty similar to ours. We benefit greatly from being with people who *know* what we are feeling.

I am quick to add, however, that in seeking out those who might be a support group for you, you need to find people who truly believe in God, believe in the power of prayer, have hope and faith alive in their hearts, and are willing to join you in praying for God to resolve your situation in a way that brings eternal reward to you and a positive witness about God's love and mercy. Don't just find a group of people to wallow in your pain with you, or join with you in "drowning your sorrows" in some kind of addictive substance. Find people who desire God's best and will join with you in persevering in faith until you receive it.

During one period in my life when I felt under extreme attack from a dishonest person who seemed intent on destroying every aspect of my life, I found that my greatest *human* solace came from a group of praying women with whom I met weekly for Bible study and Christian fellowship. They loved me in my weakest and darkest hours, and believed God with me for a miraculous turnaround. I owe much in my life today to them.

As a Christian, I know that I need *always* to stay in close fellowship with other believers, and to have at least one or two strong and mature believers who will hold me accountable. I believe this is true for all Christians. If we allow ourselves to get our eyes off the Lord and what He commands and desires, we can find ourselves in a huge mess. While I may not understand *exactly* why people make the choices they make, I do know this—it only takes opening the door a fraction of an inch for the enemy of our souls to find a way in!

I also know—if we don't make godly decisions, we *will* reap the consequences.

The Value of a Support Network

I believe it is always easier to persevere if a person remains surrounded by other people who are trusting God to produce good resolutions in their lives. God designed us as human beings to live in close fellowship with other human beings. I see this as a concept that women around the world universally understand, perhaps more so than men. They know they need their "girlfriends"—including their mothers, aunts, grandmothers, sisters, daughters, and women friends. A network of loving, supportive women can do for a woman what a man, or even a group of men, often cannot do.

Just as when choosing a good mentor, seek out and spend time with women who have:

- **Hope.** Choose to develop a deep fellowship relationship with people who are very well aware that this life is over very quickly and eternity lasts forever. Seek out those who know that they are on their way to an eternal life with the Lord Jesus Christ, and who believe that Jesus meant what He said when He told His disciples, "I am with you always, even to the end of the age." (See Matthew 28:20.) Hope is at the foundation of all genuine optimism. Your future not only *can* be better, but if you are a follower of Christ Jesus, your future *will* be better. There is a bright eternity awaiting you!

- **Faith.** Choose to associate with people who are not naïve or blindly optimistic, but rather, trust that God can and *will* help them through their current circumstance and bring them to a good outcome. They believe God's Word is *true*. They believe God's Holy Spirit is ever available and utterly trustworthy. They believe in miracles, large and small. They approach each new day with a sense of excitement to see what God has for them and others that will carry them forward and upward.

- **Love.** Surround yourself with people who are not self-serving, but rather, are generous in giving—spiritually, emotionally, materially. A true friend—and a true prayer partner, spiritual mentor, or encourager—is someone who has *your* best interests at heart. This person is not swayed by what *you* want, which frankly, sometimes is beneficial only to you and to nobody else This loving faithful person wants *God's* best for you at all times and in all ways.

God desires not only that you are relieved, helped, or blessed, but that all others impacted by your situation or circumstance are also relieved, helped, or blessed. He alone can engineer a "total package" of healing, provision, or blessing for the *whole* of your life. He is the author of all true win-win outcomes.

The Bible tells us that faith, hope, and love are God's gifts to us as believers in Christ Jesus. They are the abiding foundation for all God wants us to experience in this life. We, however, bear the responsibility of generating or "rekindling" our faith, hope, and love. Even when we feel very weak, totally inadequate, extremely vulnerable, or deeply discouraged … we *can* and *MUST* dig down deep and declare before the Lord, "I can do all things through Christ Jesus who strengthens me. I will trust You. I *will* choose to believe in You, hope for what You are going to bring my way, and love every person I encounter today." (See Philippians 4:13.)

God Will Use Your Support Team to Teach You

I realize that it is very difficult when you are in great emotional pain to see that your circumstances can *teach you* and *strengthen you*, but if you can dry your tears long enough and begin to ask God to reveal to you *what it is that you are supposed to learn* through your tragedy, I believe you will begin to heal in a way you may not have known prior to that moment.

How can you begin to *learn* what God wants you to learn in any situation? Start by asking the Holy Spirit to teach you. Jesus said He was going to send a Comforter to His disciples—and He called that Comforter our divine COUNSELOR and the SPIRIT OF TRUTH.

The Holy Spirit functions in us to say "yes" or "no" to various decisions we face in life. He functions to give us new ideas and new insights into God's Word. He functions to make us extremely sensitive to what is good and what is evil. He functions to reveal truth from lies, and to do some very specific things:

- To show us how the Bible truths might be applied to our everyday circumstances
- To give us greater knowledge about what is happening
- To give us wisdom to know how God wants us to respond to life

- To reveal the identity of negative forces of evil that might be coming against us
- To enhance or build up our faith and to believe for genuine wholeness
- To use our prayers to bring healing and encouragement to others
- To produce miracles in us and through us
- To make us more effective communicators at precisely the right moments for maximum impact
- To remind us about the nature of God and the wonderful works of God past, present, and in the future!

The Holy Spirit is our unending, continually flowing source of love, joy, peace, patience, kindness, mercy, forgiveness, and faithfulness. It is the Holy Spirit who gives us the "will" to trust His power and produce in us genuine willpower.

The Holy Spirit can teach you things that no person can teach you. He will always use the life and ministry of Jesus, and the words of the Bible, to guide you.

The Holy Spirit is our key to genuine "Bible study" and to having an effective prayer life that brings us ever closer to God.

He asks only that we come to Him and say, "Holy Spirit of Almighty God, I want more of You in my life. I want to do things Your way, not my way."

That is a prayer God always answers if we are sincere in our request.

How do I KNOW these truths?

Well … I've *lived* them.

3

My Personal Faith Journey

A friend was once asked, "How did you become a Christian?" She responded, "My parents raised me to become a Christian. Then later in life I evaluated for myself what they had taught me and I came to a conclusion that they were right."

That pretty much sums up my story, as well. I was raised in a Christ-centered home with parents who were very involved in a Christian church and who sought to apply the principles of Jesus and the Bible to their everyday lives.

My first spiritual memory was in Philadelphia. While my father was in the immigration service, we lived in that city for a couple of years. I remember a time with my family that we called "family altar." I was probably only about three years old.

Family altar was a daily bedtime ritual for us. We all knelt by the sofa as Daddy read from the Bible and then we prayed individually.

On that particular night, my younger sister and I were playing with our kitty and Dad insisted that I put the cat outside the house while we had our family spiritual time. The cat was a distraction and Dad didn't want anything to distract us from the more important business of learning God's Word and communicating with God. I remember that instance, in part, because my little cat was attacked by a larger animal outside the house, and it was injured badly and died the next morning.

Throughout my childhood, my parents emphasized Scripture memory to my sister Barbara and me. Even as a very young child, I was given verses to memorize and recite.

When I was five, I was in my first Christian pageant at church. Mother rehearsed with Barbara and me every night for several weeks. When the time came for me to say my lines before the church audience, I started out and then stopped and said, "Oh shoot, that's Barbara's part." The people laughed, I was embarrassed, and I don't think they even heard "my" lines. Barbara, of course, struggled to have composure to say *her* lines that had already been mostly said! After the performance, my mother had a little reception for some of our friends and during that time, she asked for silence so I could recite "my part," and the adults in the room would know that I was capable of saying my lines, not just Barbara's lines.

As children, Barbara and I were something of a "team of two." We didn't always blend in with the other children at school—to a great extent because of the strict behavioral boundaries associated with the church my parents attended. We couldn't go to movies, or to dances. All of our activities were church-based. We were in church Sunday morning, Sunday evening, and Wednesday evening. And if special events were planned by the church—for the entire church or for the youth—we were *there*!

In retrospect, I admire my parents for being very involved in whatever activities we participated in. They made the church activities fun for us, and as much as possible, they always included us in the planning and decorating for those events.

When I was about six, I saw a policeman walking down the street one day, and nearby was a woman wearing bright red lipstick. I asked my mother, "Why isn't that policeman giving that woman a ticket for wearing lipstick?" I knew it was against the church "rules" to wear lipstick, and I knew policemen were there to enforce the "rules." I learned that day that there are different kinds of "laws"—there is the law of the land and the law of God, and in our case, the laws associated with our church denomination. Some of those laws overlapped, of course, but not all of them. It was a little bit of a challenge to keep it all straight.

There were lots of "don't do's" in my life. We were taught that behavior and appearance were very important so that others might be won to Jesus as their Savior and not "stumble" over our bad example or sin. In spite of the strictness of the church we attended I am grateful for the boundaries and safeguards. I needed them. What I remember most are the hymns which held such great themes of truth. I still sing them today.

I was well into my thirties before I fully came to *believe* that I could ask God for His forgiveness without going forward to the altar rail at a church. In my growing-up years, there were two times a year when the church had special services—usually called revivals—and people who had sinned were invited to come forward, confess their sins, and be forgiven. It became deeply engrained in me that the altar was the designated *place* for forgiveness. What a freeing thing to realize that God could hear my confession and forgive me in any place, at any time—what mattered was the state of my heart, not the place that I knelt. My spiritual life ended up being something of a roller coaster—there was a constant "up" that came with forgiveness and an inevitable "down" that came with my mistakes, errors, and sins, and the resulting feelings of guilt.

I went to a church-based college and became involved in a church as an adult, playing the organ and leading a choir. It wasn't until I heard Bill Bright say in a Campus Crusade meeting being held at our church that things changed for me. Dr. Bright said, "Forgiveness is like this: It is like spiritual breathing. You exhale your sin and you inhale forgiveness." The light dawned. It was a shocking realization, but incredibly freeing. I knew 1 John 1:9, which says that if we confess our sins, God is faithful and just to forgive us. I just had never thought about the entire process being ongoing, and not bound to a particular church service or altar call.

A couple of years later I went to a Bible study at an office building in Pasadena. The invitation was given to us to attend a special service on Saturday. I went alone.

While at this service, I suddenly heard all of the people around me singing in a wide variety of languages. I knew that I was hearing a multitude of languages, being sung in a beautiful and well-organized harmony, and yet nobody had any music hymnals or sheet music. I looked around and realized that I knew some of the people who were singing, and I knew with certainty that they didn't know any language beyond English. I was told that the people were "singing in the Spirit" and I was asked if I wanted to be able to sing in this way. If so, I should go to a designated room after the service for prayer.

I went. I received prayer from a man who was later a Bible professor at a well-known Christian university. Almost instantly after he prayed, I found myself praying aloud in a language I had not learned but that was a definite language and distinctively "Beverly." I received instruction about this language being the kind of language described in the book of Acts. I knew this experience was real, and I left the meeting that night feeling more joy and enthusiasm about following Jesus Christ than I had ever had.

My family and friends were upset. They believed this kind of manifestation was of the devil, not God. I was "ganged up on" by a group of people in high positions in my church denomination, who did their best to get me to renounce what I had experienced. I refused. I said, "If this is *not* of God, why do I have greater feelings of love and joy related to God than I have ever experienced before?" I intuitively knew that I had a God-given right to embrace and "own" my personal experience, and the more I learned that it was an experience described by strong Christians in a number of places in the Bible, the more I felt validation for what had happened to me.

One day shortly after that, I was typing my husband's class roster, and I began to pray for the students whose names had been given to me to alphabetize and put on an attendance form. I knew the specific names of those who were in my husband's fifth period gym class. A number of them were from other nations. This was the time of forced integration in the schools and Los Angeles was a city of many nationalities and races. I thought, "The best way to pray for these kids is to pray in the Spirit like I prayed at that prayer meeting."

My husband came home that afternoon and said, "I don't know what happened but my fifth period class was amazing. The students were quiet and cooperative and attentive…."

God was beginning to show me how practical this new way of praying would be.

That summer we went camping and a couple who had gone with us suddenly began packing up. We asked why and the man said, "We have to go home. My wife lost her glasses when we were out in the boat yesterday, and she can't see a thing without them."

I said, "Oh, don't worry, and don't go yet. My husband will find those glasses."

Well, she had lost them in the waters of Yellowstone Lake, and while my husband is a good swimmer and had a good pair of goggles, the lake is fairly large and the water was very cold. Nonetheless, I said to him, "You can go out and find those glasses. I am going to pray that the Holy Spirit will show you exactly where they are."

He went, although I'm not at all sure he *believed* what I said to him. Later, he told me that while he was out in the boat, he felt prompted to go to one particular area, and he began to dive down the twelve to fourteen feet toward the bottom of that part of the lake, and sure enough, he found that pair of glasses!

Another example of God's kindness and grace to me occurred one day as I was sitting at my kitchen table and looking over all the bills knowing I couldn't pay them. I cried out to God and said: "God, I need $1,000 today to meet these expenses." Not long after that there was a knock at my door. My dear friend Eloise was there and said, "I was drying dishes and the Lord spoke to me and said, 'Go, give Beverly $1,000.' So here I am." I began to cry and told her about my urgent prayer. We rejoiced together.

That very day in the mail came a letter from Corrie ten Boom in reply to a letter I had sent to her quite a while earlier telling her how I admired her bravery and trust in God. It read:

> Thank you so much for getting in touch with me. You probably came to hear about me through seeing the film, *The Hiding Place,* or reading one of my books. Did you understand that there was a message in it for you?
>
> I myself learned through the experiences described that when the worst happens in the life of a child of God, the best remains. Yes, no pit is so deep that the everlasting arms of the Lord are not deeper still. I learned the difference between the security of the world and the security of the Lord. Heaven and earth will pass away; God's Word will never pass away.
>
> In Jesus the Victor, (signed) Corrie ten Boom

The Double-Edged Sword of Leadership

I had always been a leader, in school, business, at church, wherever. It didn't take long for people to see I was capable and willing. I wasn't always wise.

Leadership is a great responsibility. Leadership without counsel is dangerous. We all need accountability and wise counsel. Close friends and those we trust can often help us to make much better decisions than we would make on our own.

My husband wanted to move to Oregon and leave the big city life. We had just adopted our precious daughter, Debi. I had resigned from all my various responsibilities to stay at home and be her mom. It was such a blessing. My family was all close around and things were going well, but he wanted to move so we did. It was a very difficult decision to pick up and start over.

Upon our arrival in Oregon my husband wanted to attend a small church in our denomination. Again, we are in an atmosphere where I didn't have the opportunity to learn more about the gifts of the Holy Spirit and how to grow in them. I determined not to become a leader again in yet another church. I wanted my husband to lead, not me. However, after a few months the people in that little church we attended discovered I could play the piano ... and so it began. More and more responsibilities were piled on my plate. I ended up directing the choir, producing musicals for the children, playing the piano and organ, and leading the women's ministry. Working for the King is not the same as abiding with the King and listening for His direction.

If anyone would have said to me, "You are headed for divorce," I would have replied, "no way!" But if you do things on your own and don't think you need anyone to give you caution, you can fail in a dramatic way!

The best thing about moving to Oregon was that we adopted Paul when he was three days old. What a blessing he was to me and to our family! He was a contented, jolly baby and he loved to laugh at his sister's antics.

When Paul was six and Debi was eleven we moved back to California. Money was tight and I had been offered a teaching position in the music department at a college in southern California.

My husband and I had started a business on the side, but we were really struggling. In hindsight, I can see clearly how financial difficulties can get a person's eyes off the Source of all provision, and lead a person to start believing he or she can—even *must*—solve those financial problems on their own strength. Again, leadership without counsel and accountability isn't wise leadership, or maybe no leadership at all. If you are reading this and identify with this scenario, please get professional counseling. Usually things can be worked out but we each have to humble ourselves and seek help.

A business can be a twofold challenge: On the one hand, you have opportunities you never had before, and on the other hand, you have responsibilities you never had either. Greed, power, and illicit relationships are common temptations, which the enemy of our soul uses quite effectively.

We must never forget that the devil is like a lion stalking us, seeking whom he may devour. (See 1 Peter 5:8.)

I got devoured.

My husband and I divorced and agreed on joint custody of the children. How very, very difficult that was! After several years we both remarried and moved to different locations. All of this took a heavy toll on our children. I have tried to warn so many couples since then who are considering divorce that it is almost *impossible* for children to move forward in a positive way after a divorce. Again, counseling with Christian psychologists and professionals could have made a difference.

Several years after my former husband remarried, I also remarried, but after some very stormy years, that second marriage also ended in divorce.

I suspect that I am like all women who have troubled marriages and go through long, drawn-out, and messy divorce proceedings. The pain is intense. Regardless of all the details associated with the relationship— which are really nobody's business but everybody's fuel for gossip—the residual effect seems always to be one of feeling shattered, betrayed, maligned and mistreated, unfairly judged, rejected, and wounded in ways one never thought imaginable. There is always a tremendous sense of *loss*—sometimes financial, always personal. There is often a major hit to one's self-esteem and overall reputation. There is a prevailing feeling of injustice. I've experienced it all, and with such pain that I simply don't care to recall those days and emotions.

I know two things: One, time does *not* heal. Only God heals. Time may fade a memory or two, but it does not mend the human heart. Only God can do that. And two: Only God can fully avenge the pain a person causes another person. God tells us to leave all vengeance to Him. I'm willing to do that.

When my second marriage fell apart, I vowed I'd never marry again. I told my children I would just be with them and try not to mess up their lives any more. I asked their forgiveness many times over. They were gracious and received my multitude of apologies. The pain, however, was always with them, and that, in turn, meant my pain *for* them was always there, as well.

Through all these years of trouble I continued to build business domestically and internationally with some good success. But success isn't enough.

I struggled with many emotions that I have seen repeatedly in others who have come to me in *their* pain through the years since that time. Some are overwhelmed with feelings of failure and rejection. Some are scared as they look into their future ... and some are scared of their abusive or unfaithful husbands, who seem to be able to wield public opinion in their favor, and wrangle all business decisions to their favor. Some are very sad, fearing that they have let their children down. Some are so discouraged and emotionally worn down that they can't even imagine having energy to continue their business, much less think of starting a new business or expanding their business. Some are questioning their faith ... or their ability to discern ... or their judgment ... or their own identity as a woman. Some feel forlorn that they might never find a man who will love them tenderly and genuinely. Some feel exceedingly vulnerable. Some feel weak, to the point of feeling they have almost no self-value or self-esteem.

I experienced all of those emotions and more, to some degree, at some time in my divorce-recovery process.

Although I had been miserable in the marriage, I was nonetheless devastated when things fell apart. I took my Bible, a copy of *Experiencing God* by Henry Blackaby, and went by myself to Hawaii for three weeks to rest, think, and most of all, pray. I knew that I was not experiencing the relationship I longed to have with the Lord, and that I needed to rekindle my love for Him, first and foremost.

In that book Henry explains how important it is not to just say to God: "Bless my plans." He encourages us to "Observe where God is working and go and be there." What a concept. I had never done that before.

A Life-Altering Meeting

While still in Hawaii, I went to a meeting that was devoted to Bible-based teaching about and actual expressions of the "gifts" of the Spirit as described in 1 Corinthians 12 of the New Testament. I knew that I had a relationship with the Holy Spirit, but I did not know the full extent of what that relationship might involve.

The conference was promoted as a "prophecy" seminar. I went thinking that the meeting would be about prophecy as it related to the "end times" and the "second coming of Christ." No—it was a conference about the "gift of prophecy" described by St. Paul in his writings to the Corinthian church.

Nobody knew me at the meeting. Not even my name. I was a stranger in their midst.

As part of the meeting, various ones began to speak words *about* others around them. These were encouraging words and they were spoken with spiritual authority. To my surprise, the people *receiving* these words were not resistant to or defensive about what was being said. Rather, they gave affirmation that what was spoken was *true*, and the words were good words of wisdom and direction for their life.

Then it came to be *my* turn for someone to speak about me. The person said, "The Lord saw you when you were on your pillow as you lay on your face on your bedroom floor and cried out to God. He heard you. He wants you to know that He still has a wonderful future for you. He is going to raise you up and heal you and send you around the world to be a witness for Him in ways you have not imagined. And you will not go alone, but you will be part of a team of people." Another person said, "You will show women in many nations that they are valuable to the Lord." Yet another spoke up, "God is going to show people that a woman can do things in a man's world."

As they were speaking, I kept thinking, "How could they possibly know this? I was face down on my bedroom floor with my head on a little pillow crying out to God."

Truly, the God who knew where the glasses were at the bottom of Yellowstone Lake also knew where Beverly was!

The Bible says the *Lord* is the husband of widows and orphans. It is a difficult but a wonderful thing to realize that you can count on GOD HIMSELF to provide for you and protect you just as a good and loving husband seeks to provide for and protect his wife.

I was amazed, in awe, and in a way that is difficult to describe, I was invigorated and renewed in my innermost being. These people had no "reason" to say what they said to me. They had no information about my current struggles and self-doubts. They had no facts related to my discouragement or feelings of rejection or dashed dreams and goals. They were simply being obedient to the Holy Spirit and were speaking what they truly believed *He* desired to say to me, through them.

That night changed everything for me. It gave me a new understanding about how much God cared for me, and how tenderly and gently He wanted me to know that He loved me and was going to take care of me. At the same time, it gave me a new understanding about how powerful prayer can be, and that there is nothing and nobody who is as powerful and life-giving as the Holy Spirit of Almighty God.

I had a relationship with God through Jesus Christ. I had a relationship with the Holy Spirit. But that night, I yielded my entire life to a *dependency* upon God in a way that I had never before "given" myself to the Lord.

I became involved with a couple who had built a very fine networking business, and an especially strong network of associates in Australia. They invited me to be a part of their team. Truly, I wasn't going to embark on a worldwide effort on my own!

Years later, I thanked the husband of this couple for his constant encouragement and motivating words. His wife interjected, "My husband loved you and encouraged you. But I loved you and prayed for you!" Prayer and encouragement in the context of love—what a wonderful thing that is!

I began lines of business in India and South Africa within the next twelve months. They were busy days. And successful days.

I learned that every nation had different rules for conducting business. I needed to learn those rules. But, the one constant seemed to be that *relationship* is the key to international business regardless of nationality or culture.

The team of which I was a part understood the importance of relationship and their basic business model called for the team to develop a relationship with people from a foreign nation who were currently living in the United States. They are usually called "ex-pats"— and they may be actual citizens of the USA now, or in many cases, people who are here on work visas or in the process of immigration to become citizens. These ex-pats know people from their homeland, and they know people who know people. If a group in the USA sponsored us to a foreign nation, we found that we could put together an audience and find a venue in another nation, and go there with a very basic understanding on the part of the foreign audience that we were "friends"—we were honorable people doing respectable work. Our products were top quality and the opportunity we offered was genuine. We had a starting point for integrity and honest business dealings, and then it was up to us to build on that and to attract people to our business model who were also people of integrity and honesty.

This entire way of doing business fit me like a shoe made precisely for my foot!

My Advice about Marriage

Some people have asked me through the years, "Are you 'down' on marriage?"

Not at all!

Through the years, I have been quick to invite well-recognized and respected marriage counselors to various large meetings I have sponsored. I have told these counselors, "Please help people not to make the mistakes I made." I tell my audiences, "These people are here to help YOU to avoid my mistakes." And at most of these events, I have helped individual couples arrange personalized counseling sessions. I want to see marriages made strong, or grow stronger. That is better for the family as a whole. It is ultimately better for the business, although whether the business fails or succeeds, it is far more important to me that the marriage and family succeed!

I made it very clear that I was not interested in a woman leaving her husband or abandoning or shortchanging her children.

Many women were shocked when I said to them, "I was twice divorced before I learned some of the principles I'm going to share with you." I have no doubt they paid more attention to the advice I gave than if I had swept my failures under the carpet and pretended that I had lived a perfect life.

With my failures, of course, came the information that I had *overcome* many of the negative consequences of my failures by putting my trust in God. They often expected me to say that I crawled out from under the sadness, financial loss, and family loss in my life by my own intellect, hard work, or ambition. I didn't downplay the need for thinking smart, working hard, or desiring more. But I also gave supreme credit to the Lord—I didn't *make* or *remake* myself. God made me, and He remade me, and He continues to remake me for His purposes and for His honor!

I do my part, trusting Him to do what only *He* can do. I cannot do what God does. He doesn't expect me to do His part. But at the same time, He won't do my part. He wants my trust and devotion, my love and praise. I must give to God what pleases Him. Not in anticipation of His favor, but because He is my Creator and He is the One who is in charge of all things, all the time. I live for Him and I exist to bring Him pleasure.

One of the ways I know I am in the presence of a true Christian is this: I ask, "When did Jesus become personal to you?"

If the person begins to tell me all that they believe God is going to do for them, I know they don't truly understand their position before God or their dependence on Him.

We exist for God. He doesn't exist for us.

He is in charge. We aren't.

The Bible is very clear on this. Those who draw near to God are the ones to whom God draws near. He wants a relationship with us, and that relationship is rooted in a flow of mutual love and a deep and abiding awe that Jesus Christ is the "King of the Universe." He governs everything and all things exist because of Him and for Him.

I often sign my correspondence, "In the King," or "For the King," or "Because of the King." Everything I do—in business and in my personal life—must bring honor to the King for it to have genuine and lasting value. Nothing exists except that He allows it. Nothing grows except what *He* grows. Nothing lasts except what He authorizes.

If a person catches hold of those truths, and applies those truths to her life *and to her business*, there's nothing that can stand in her way from doing more, being more, and ultimately, having more—including more satisfaction, fulfillment, and joy!

In some of the meetings I sponsored, I invited a well-known marriage counselor, Dr. David Beighley, to speak. David had become a close friend and the wise counselor I had needed for so long.

From what I learned through David, as well as other speakers and counselors through the years, there is a key to making a marriage work—one I did not learn in my early years and one that I am quick to share. That key is summed up in the word *FORGIVE*.

4

Forgiveness: The Key to Moving Beyond Personal Heartache

Seventeen years after my second divorce, which took considerable time to "untangle" financially, I met Arthur. I found in him a man who was investing his time and energy into the lives of young people and inner-city people in need. I had never met anyone like him. We developed a wonderful friendship, over time.

The key words there are *friendship* and *over time*.

As I indicated earlier, I initially promised my children that I would not remarry. I was committed to a single life. I was grateful that I had an opportunity to live for a period of time with both of my children after they were adults and before they married. We learned to relate to each other in new and deeper ways, and I will be forever thankful to the Lord for that.

I knew that before I could ever enter any type of romantic relationship with a man, I would need to spend considerable time praying about that, and making absolutely certain that it is what the Lord wanted for my life.

And then along came Arthur. He was a retired dentist who lived in Michigan, and who knew a number of people in my business who also lived in Michigan. We met and as years passed, our "acquaintanceship" became a genuine mutually-caring friendship.

When Arthur said to me while we were sitting in Starbucks one day, "Beverly, would you let me love you?" I was surprised to the point that I could scarcely respond. I blurted out, "You would consider a twice-divorced woman?"

He replied, "Well, did God forgive you?"

I said, "Yes."

He said, "Well if God has forgiven you, what are you talking about? What is the problem?"

I had never encountered someone who was willing to forgive me *as God has forgiven me.*

I went to my hotel room that night and asked the Lord, "What is this all about?"

The Lord spoke directly into my spirit, "I have sent this man to heal you." I knew in an instant that God had sent Arthur into my life and it was for *His* purposes. I had such a deep dependency on the Lord at that time, God's opinion was the only opinion that *truly* mattered to me. If God approved of Arthur, who was I to question someone *He* had sent to me?

Forgiveness Is a Powerful KEY

I learned a great deal from Corrie ten Boom in a book she wrote that recounted a profound outpouring of God's help so she might forgive the Nazi who had imprisoned her and her sister in a concentration camp, where her sister died.

She underscored for me the great importance of forgiveness to a person's spiritual health—not only receiving forgiveness from God but also forgiving others who have hurt us.

Through the years, I have met many people who are filled with emotions that may not manifest themselves *all* the time, but when they do erupt, they erupt like a volcano! Lack of forgiveness is often at the foundation of the negativity and pain they spew all over every person in the sound of their voice.

How do you know if you need to forgive? The residual and outward symptoms of unforgiveness are usually anger, hatred, and bitterness, which are fairly easy to recognize.

Anger is something the Bible tells us that we can feel but that we are never to let our anger "last." In fact, the Bible says we should get rid of it before we go to sleep at night. The godly purpose of anger is to motivate us to right a wrong, or to seek to overturn an injustice. A little anger is like the trigger to put us in motion to take action against something that *should be addressed and changed*. It is a good thing, for example, to get angry when we see a child abused, a case of extreme poverty allowed to continue, or a situation in which a corrupt judge or politician "uses" people for his own advancement in power. There are many ways to channel our anger so that it can produce a good outcome—we are wise to seek those avenues and pursue them!

Bitterness occurs when we continue to rehearse a wrong we think has been done to us. We dwell on it and allow it to sink deep into our soul. Like unresolved anger, it can begin to seethe within us to the point that we openly display resentment toward a person or people that we believe will *always* be against us, never neutral about us or in favor of our existence.

Hatred is often linked to blind prejudice, a long history of being abused, or a deep feeling of being rejected or overlooked unfairly.

The point I want to make is this: longstanding anger, bitterness, resentment, and hatred do *nothing* for us. They do not make us stronger, healthier, or more appealing. In fact, scientific studies are showing more and more that these emotions are correlated to poor health, even deadly diseases.

Furthermore, most people do not enjoy being around people who are consistently negative—and especially so, those who *always* seem to be angry, bitter, resentful, or hateful. My contention is that negative emotions are inconsistent with business success.

What should a person do to move their innermost feelings from negative to positive? I believe the key is forgiveness.

Forgiveness is *not* saying that something didn't happen (when it did). It is not saying that the hurtful event or relationship didn't matter (it did, and may still). It is not saying that justice should not be pursued (it may be to the benefit of many people).

Forgiveness, in its purest form, is "letting go." It is saying, "I will not hold this person or this relationship or this memory in the cage of my heart. I will release it." Most people find it even more powerful if they say, "I choose to let go, and let God." Those who simply let go of a painful experience, as if sending it off in some vague way to the end of the galaxy, do not find forgiveness nearly as healing as those who say, "I choose to put this person and this situation into God's hands and trust Him to mete out His justice." We can count on God's justice always to be healing to the person who has been hurt. Knowing that "God is in charge" frees a person from seeking revenge, and it allows a person to turn all of their mental and emotional energy toward people and projects that are worthy of their creativity, compassion, and communication.

Some people say, "I just *can't* forgive. The grievance is too great."

The truth is, "Every person *can* forgive." Forgiveness does not enable a person to resolve their own pain—rather, it turns that pain over to God who *can* resolve it.

The greater the offense, the greater the need to lay it down and not pick it up again! The more intense the hurt, the more important it is that a person live free of it!

Some people say, "I will try to forgive, but I'll never forget." The truth is that we can never truly forget *anything*. God has given us our memory so we *will* remember bad things and never do them again or seek to acquire them, and remember good things so we *will* do them or seek more of them in our lives. God never asks us to forget. He does *command* us to forgive. In fact, the command is so strong that God says we must forgive other people if we want God to forgive us.

Jesus is quoted in the New Testament as saying, "To whom much is given, from him much will be required." (Luke 12:48) Many people seem to think that statement relates to the use of talents, or the giving of material possessions or money. I believe it means, first and foremost, giving *forgiveness*. When we are aware that we have been forgiven by God, and have a glimpse into all that our forgiveness from God means to us now and in eternity, we surely must feel *compelled* to forgive others. Many people's reply to Luke 12:48 is, "To whom much is forgiven, Jesus is ALL that's required!" Jesus forgives completely, and we must seek to do the same.

I also want to point out that forgiveness sometimes doesn't occur by saying glibly on one occasion, "I forgive you." A person may need to forgive a person again and again and again—in fact, perhaps at every recurrence of memory about a particular incident or conversation. Time doesn't heal—not really—but repeated forgiveness over time usually does bring a person to the point where the pain is gone and the memory fades, and the person is no longer limited or trapped in a prison of anger, bitterness, resentment, or hatred.

I also have made it a point to be *quick* to forgive. Any time a person comes to mind with the thought, "I hurt that person," or even, "I *may* have hurt that person," I have done my best to go to that person and say, "Please forgive me."

Even if the person *doesn't* forgive me, I have a freedom in my heart that comes from asking for their forgiveness.

I don't ask for forgiveness after I have made excuses or offered justifications for what I did or didn't do. There's no excuse that is ever adequate, and very often, the "reasons" I may have acted badly were rooted in the behavior of others long ago. There's no advantage at all in bringing them into a conversation or relationship! No—I must take full responsibility for what I have done, and ask for forgiveness expecting nothing in return and offering no excuses. Only then is the forgiveness pure and only then does forgiveness set a person free.

The more I forgive others freely, the more freedom I feel in my heart, and the more courage I have to ask for forgiveness, *and to forgive myself.* Sometimes the most difficult person to forgive is yourself! It is only when we forgive ourselves that we truly can move forward in life with a boldness and freedom that is beyond explanation to those who are still bound up in unforgiveness.

I also have made no excuses for the failures in my marriages. Frankly, the details are nobody's business. And just as frankly, the details are nothing I care to bring back into the cage of my own mind and heart. I don't want to revisit the pain or the circumstances that gave rise to the pain. Forgiveness frees me from *rehearsing*, or revisiting, the past. First Peter 3:11 (NLT), "Turn away from evil and do good. Search for peace, and work to maintain it."

In Sweden while conducting a series of meetings a couple asked me to visit a woman who had terminal cancer. I got alone with her and asked her if she read the Bible very much. She said, "No." I said, "May I show a verse to you in the Bible?" She said, "Yes." I opened my Bible to her and read John 3:16, "For God so loved the world, that he gave his only begotten Son, that whosoever believeth in him should not perish, but have everlasting life." I explained to her that if she ever wanted a relationship with God, all she had to do was say, "Thank You for loving me. I believe Jesus is Your only Son, and I ask that You forgive me for everything I have done that has been contrary to Your commands or to Your will for me." We talked a few minutes about forgiveness and I assured her that God can forgive ANYTHING. It doesn't matter how great our sin has been or how many times we have sinned. He wants to forgive us and be in a loving relationship with us. And, He desires that we forgive others, too.

She prayed a simple prayer with me and I left.

I learned that in the next several days after we had met and prayed, she met with her children, one by one, and several others, including her estranged husband, and asked them to forgive her. They did, and in turn, asked her to forgive them. She did. And ... she died about a month later. Her husband was with her in the hospital every day during the final hours of her life.

God will use us if we are willing to listen to His voice and obey His leading.

Release from Inner Pain

It took me years to forgive my enemies. I clung to the words of Jesus in Matthew 5 that we are to bless our enemies, and pray for those who spitefully use you and persecute you. One day, a business enemy of mine came down a staircase that I was ascending and there was nothing I could do but come face to face with him. He greeted me as if nothing had ever been wrong between us. I responded, "I am praying for you." That was all I could get out. But that, for me, was obeying what Jesus said to do.

In saying that, something was released inside me. I *did* forgive, although I didn't use the word *forgive*. What I said released the person from *my* heart.

The Bible verse on which I depended greatly in those days was Proverbs 22:1, which says, "A good name is rather to be chosen than great riches."

If the Lord brought anybody to my mind with the thought, "You need to forgive that person," I humbled myself and went to them and asked for forgiveness. If the Lord called me to walk boldly, especially in areas or about things that I had not done and had been falsely accused of doing ... well, I walked boldly. I was intent on upholding my own integrity and good name, and I refused to allow others to drag me down into their pit of lies and deceit.

Not only have I come to a position where I feel very free in asking forgiveness of others, but I also believe there is great impact possible when we pronounce God's forgiveness to others who are desperate to know that God desires to, can, and does forgive them!

In Brazil I spoke for some meetings where a German couple were my interpreters. They had come to Brazil after World War II and had built a successful language school there. After our weekend together, as Otto was driving me back to my hotel, I suddenly felt prompted in my spirit to say to him, "Otto, I want you to know that there is nothing that you did during the war that Jesus didn't die for two thousand years ago. He died so you can be completely forgiven."

I wasn't quite prepared for the response. Otto had stopped his car by this time and he slumped over the steering wheel and cried like a baby. Something was released deep in his spirit.

I suggested that he meet with a minister who was part of our conference and who was staying in the same hotel where I was staying. I didn't feel that I should be the one to counsel this man, but I did sense he needed to confess fully his sins and pray with someone who would further assure him of God's forgiveness. I was grateful when he told me later that he had met with this man and was very grateful for that evening in his life.

5

The Major Disciplines that
Keep Me in Focus

U sing Skype and other means of messaging, I have had an
opportunity to converse with a number of business associates
around the world in an ongoing way. Many of these are
women who request my counsel not only in their business, but in their
personal lives. Some come from Christian backgrounds and have a basic
understanding of the Bible and of Jesus, but many don't. In fact, some
of the young women that I correspond with or communicate with on
Skype have grown up in other religions. Nevertheless, they have a
spiritual hunger and they have seen something of a spiritual nature in
me that they want to explore for themselves.

For the most part, these women have come to trust me because
they have seen how I live out my beliefs in beneficial ways to help
others.

A recurring question from many of them has been, "Beverly, what
do you do to stay on the path of your spiritual journey?" They want
practical answers that relate to everyday living.

And here is what I tell them …

The First Hour of My Day

During the last fifteen years that I traveled around the world in my business, I made a decision that I would keep to a schedule of getting up one hour before I *had* to get up in order to make a flight or show up at a particular meeting on time. As an example, if I knew that I needed to get up by seven o'clock to get ready, pack, check out, and get to the airport by nine to make an international flight that left at eleven … I set my alarm to get up at SIX o'clock. I trusted God to give that hour back to me for sleep while I was in the air.

There have been a couple of times when I calculated that I needed to get up at two o'clock in the morning, and by the time I was making this calculation it was already midnight. Well … I set my alarm for 1 AM. I got an hour of sleep, and in those instances, I am glad to report that the flights were long enough that I got several hours of sleep while I was flying at 30,000 plus feet in a first-class seat on a comfortable jet.

What do I do in that hour?

First and foremost, I read my Bible *out loud* and sometimes other Christian devotional material, and I pray. I talk to God, and I listen to God. We have a dialog, not just a monolog of my voicing my concerns or requests. I want to learn what God is thinking, what God wants to do in my life and the lives of others, and how God wants me to spend the upcoming day and handle various appointments that I am facing. I want this hour with the Lord to be unhurried and yet focused. This first hour of my day is an hour that I desire to have *alone* with God. It is an hour that I set aside to be *all ABOUT God*.

There is tremendous power in reading the Bible out loud. The devil doesn't stick around to hear God's Word! I say aloud, "I submit to You, God. I resist you, devil … you *must* flee. In the Name of Jesus Christ of Nazareth, I cast you out of this room and out of my life. Only the Spirit of God can dwell in me and in this room. None of your dark spirits will be allowed here!" (See James 4:7.)

I not only pray this as I'm preparing to read the Scriptures, but I often pray this as soon as I enter into a hotel room with my luggage. There's no telling what has gone on in that room prior to my arrival there. I want to clean out any residual evil presence that may be lingering in that room! There have been times when I had a strong palpable sense that evil left the scene and the Holy Spirit flooded into that space.

Personal "Favorite Passages" from the Bible. Let me share a few of the passages of Scripture that have meant the most to me down through the years, and across the face of the earth. I am giving you only the "references" for these Scriptures. I encourage every woman to find and use a version of the Bible that she enjoys reading—it should be a version that is easy for her to understand, and if the particular edition has study notes embedded in it, all the better!

- **Isaiah 25:1–6** is sometimes labeled in some Bible versions as "a song of praise by the redeemed."
- **John 14–17**. These chapters are filled with the final words of Jesus. They are powerful and filled with love. I often read these chapters aloud, one chapter after the next.
- **Psalm 116.**
- **Psalm 45.**
- **The Song of Solomon**. I love to read this book, and to do so as if I am reading a novel, or perhaps even as a love letter between God and me. I especially enjoy reading it in the Amplified Version of the Bible.
- **Revelation 17 and Revelation 19**. These two chapters in the final book of the Bible tell the glories of our eternal home!
- **Psalm 61** has been turned into a song. It has been one of my favorite songs to sing quietly to myself in airports around the world. If you have heard a woman singing this psalm in the airports of India, China, or Africa or some other remote region of the world where English is not commonly spoken, it just may have been me! The psalm begins:

> Hear my cry, O God; attend unto my prayer.
> From the end of the earth will I cry unto thee,
> when my heart is overwhelmed.
> Lead me to the rock that is higher than I;
> for thou hast been a shelter for me, and a strong tower from
> the enemy.
> (Psalm 61:1–3)

I once was detained by customs police in India and was told that I needed to pay five hundred dollars. They said that various gift items I had in my suitcase, which I was taking into India to give away to my business associates there, were items that I was planning to sell and that they were therefore subject to an import tax. I knew they were gouging me for money, but also knew that they had the authority to make my stay in India miserable and even to keep me from entering the nation. They had put me in an isolated area, and not even given the permission to make a call to the people who were outside the customs area waiting for me. I prayed to the Lord for safety and I eventually paid what they requested. But all the time, I was singing Psalm 61 under my breath! That chapter of Psalms has two wonderful phrases that are worthy of repeating often in our lives:

- "I will trust in the cover of thy wings." (Psalm 61:4)

- "I will sing praise unto thy name for ever, that I may daily perform my vows." (Psalm 61:8)

What strong statements of faith and resolve, no matter the danger!

- **Psalm 91.**

- **John 4.** The Lord showed me one day that I had a great deal in common with the woman that Jesus met at the well.

- **1 Corinthians 1.**

My Basic Reading Plan. I usually read one chapter from the Old Testament, consecutively. I read one chapter of Psalms, consecutively. I read one chapter in the New Testament, consecutively.

And then I focus on three specific areas of reading:

- *The Proverb of the "date."* In other words, if the date is the 12th of the month, I read Proverbs 12. The book of Proverbs is truly a "working manual" for the how-to practicality of a life of faith that is pleasing to God. It is a book of very concrete wisdom!

- *A portion of Psalm 119.* This psalm is divided according to the letters of the Hebrew alphabet. The word *Aleph* in Hebrew is equal to our "A" in English; *Bet* is "B" in English and so forth. There are 22 segments in Psalm 119, each of which has eight verses on a particular theme that is related to the character and identity of the Lord. As an example, the theme for the eight verses in ALEPH is "The Lord's judgments are righteous."

  I often read another of the psalms in addition to a portion of Psalm 119. The psalms (the word *psalm* literally means "song") are God's message of encouragement—a testimony that God can do everything and resolve every difficulty in life. He knows all, governs all, creates all things, and is ever-present and all-loving.

- *A statement of Jesus.* If you buy an edition of the Bible that has the words of Jesus printed in red, you'll find it easy to find His words! You may want to read an entire chapter from the Gospels (Matthew, Mark, Luke, and John).

These are areas for true *contemplation*. I ponder these words. I study them. I seek to memorize them. I look for deep and deeper meaning.

The important point, of course, is this: Read *something* from the Word of God every day. Ask God to guide your reading. And pray before you begin to read, "Lord, speak to me through Your Word." Ask God to seal what you read deep into your spirit so that you will never forget it, and that you will gain increasing understanding, a stronger faith, and a greater desire to "live out" His message to you.

Commit Scripture to Memory. I feel very bold in encouraging people to learn and memorize the Scriptures.

A young woman I had known from the time she was born, wrote to me not long ago. She is now eighteen and she asked, "Will you please tell me your favorite life verses—the verses you base your life on?" I encouraged her to memorize some key verses that she could stand on when life gets difficult. I recommended:

- Psalm 1
- Psalm 19
- Psalm 23
- Psalm 27
- Psalm 91
- Psalm 103
- 1 Peter 5:8
- James 1:5
- James 4:7

What you commit to memory is like a "Bible" that you carry with you always! It is instantly accessible!

Quoting the Bible in Conversation. I make a very conscious effort *not* to get into doctrinal disputes or discussions with people. I stand on the true foundation that God is God, and I'm not. Jesus is unique, irreplaceable, and sovereign. If a person says Jesus is anything other than God, I make my claim that I believe He *is* God, but I will not argue. I simply say, "This is what the Bible says ... and here is what that verse or passage has meant to me."

The Tremendous Value of Prayer

Prayer gives me something that some people call a "sixth sense." Some people may call it intuition, or a "sure feeling." For me, it is something spiritual that I perceive to be a direct gift from God. I often find that new ideas and impressions come to me as part of a process called "prayerful listening." That is simply a matter of praying and then listening!

- **Wisdom.** I ask God for wisdom in advance of a meeting or business counseling session. And I believe even as I ask that it is God's desire to *give* us His wise counsel. I contend we each need to be open to God's advice and receive it as an act of faith, believing that God *wants* to show us His plans and purposes, and bless us as we act on those plans and purposes. The Bible says in James 1:5–6, "If any of you lacks wisdom, let him ask of God, who gives to all liberally and without reproach, and it will be given to him. But let him ask in faith, with no doubting."
- **Help.** I usually ask the Lord before I speak or sing, "Help me to do my best." And, if I was conducting a group of young people in a concert and it was appropriate, I would say a brief prayer with them before the event, "Help us to do our best." And then I added, "We give all the results to You."
- **Renewed Energy.** I know what it means to be *exhausted*— physically and emotionally. There's nothing quite as demanding as speaking before thousands, and then counseling with individuals, hour after hour after hour.

    There was only one way that I could handle such a demanding work schedule.

    I prayed.
- **Guidance.** In my prayers, I asked God to guide me every minute of every hour of the day. I asked Him to give me insights into what to say to the large audiences. And I asked Him to reveal to me the way I might help individuals *most*. I wanted every person who came to me to know that I wanted what was best for *them*— personally, their marriage, their family, and their future.

Even before I gave any words of specific individual advice, the women knew on an individual basis that I wanted God's best *for her*. That was a very different mind-set for many women at the meetings. They lived in cultures and were involved with people who were intent only on what the woman could do for *them*—she might have a husband that was looking far more for what his wife could do for *him* rather than what he might do for *her* ... or, a supervisor at work who was intent on the quality and quantity of work that she could produce (and also how much she could increase her production) more than he was intent on ways in which she might be rewarded for good work or increased work ... or, a family that was intent on what she could provide for them—whether parents seeking her help or children needing her attention. These women often came to a session with me *expecting* to learn what I thought the woman could do for *me,* or what I was *expecting from her.* They were almost shocked at my perspective, "I am here to help *you.* I want what is best for *you.* Only you know what that is. But if I can help you in any way to live a better quality of life, I want to help you based on my experience and understanding."

A high percentage of the women who came to me for individual meetings would say to me later, "How did you know what to tell me? You said *just what I needed to hear!"*

My answer was, "I prayed."

My heart was motivated to help. And God gave me the specific information to help.

Staying Sensitive to God Sightings

Every day, I am looking almost continually for what God may be doing—either in me or around me. I am looking for instances that affirm to me, "God is at work in this world!" I am not only looking for what God is *doing,* but what He also might be asking me to do. I try always to be sensitive to how God might want me to schedule my time, arrange my meetings, or "engineer" my appointment schedule to enable certain encounters or fulfill specific purposes.

When I first went to South Africa, I asked myself, "Do I need three versions of my business talks? Do I need one for the blacks, one for the coloreds (the Indians and Asians), and one for the Afrikaners (the Dutch descendants)?" The Lord showed me I needed only *one* message and that it needed to be aimed at the *human heart.*

I decided simply to speak from *my* heart to *their* hearts. And I said to the Lord, "It is totally up to You to reveal that I am a servant of Yours and a follower of Christ Jesus."

I had one woman come to me after a presentation in South Africa, and she said, "You're a Christian, aren't you?"

I said, "Yes, but how did you know that?"

She said, "Its all over your face!"

I breathed a quiet, "Thank You, God."

Stay Focused

Do not allow yourself to become bogged down in off-track arguments. One of the enemy's foremost strategies is to get us preoccupied with all sorts of questions that don't have answers, all sorts of speculations that are not truly predictable or provable, or all sorts of arguments that are based upon differences of style or procedures (but are not truly differences on what matters to God for all eternity).

We must ask about every conversation or argument that seems to draw us a little further away from God rather than closer to God, "Will this matter five hundred years from now?" If the answer is NO, drop it.

Through the years I have heard many people spend long hours, and sometimes decades, arguing whether one method of baptism is better than another (sprinkle, pour water over the head, or immerse completely … infants or adults only … in a church or at a river … in private or public … just once and never again, or multiple times during your life). The Bible command doesn't include a methodology or time frame. It says simply, "Repent and be baptized." (See Acts 2:38 as one example.) I go with that basic command.

I've heard people spend considerable time and energy trying to predict the second coming of the Lord, and how His return will relate to a time that the Bible calls "great tribulation." They ask, when will it happen (today or a hundred years from now), how will it happen (rapture of the church or not), in what sequence will events happen (will the deliverance of the church come before, halfway through, or at the end of a tribulation period). The Bible's simplest message on this is that Jesus is coming again and we need to be ready for His return. Furthermore, there will be Christians alive and Christians who are dead and in paradise with the Lord when it happens. In sum, be ready.

I've heard people talk a great deal about whether they are to be prosperous or poor, whether they are to suffer or be healed, whether they need to belong to a church or avoid going to church, and how they can know God's will. I believe God wants us to have all that we need to fulfill what He has designed for us to be and to do on this earth, and that the "church" includes all who believe fully in Jesus as the Son of God and our Savior. God's will for us is that we love Him with all of our heart, soul, mind, and strength, and our neighbors as ourselves. Beyond that ... well, I think we should be so busy doing what we *know* to do and how to help other people find God and live in close relationship with Him, that we don't have time to worry about what others are doing or not doing!

From my perspective, the old phrase "Keep It Simple" applies to our faith and our devotion to the Lord. God has made it very simple for a person to have a relationship with Him. He says, "Believe, receive My Son, accept My forgiveness." There's no rocket science in that. He says, "I will be with you and help you." There's no one-hundred page manual we have to complete to qualify for His assistance. He says, "I love you and you can trust Me in all things. I can make a way where there doesn't seem to be a way. I know all that is required, and I'm not going to leave you where you are right now. There's more to knowing Me, more for you to become and do, and more for you to experience—now and for all eternity." I choose to take Him at His word!

6

Facing the Challenges of Life—
Big and Small

H ave I ever been fooled by people?

Have I ever been disappointed by people I trusted?

Have I ever "misread" a person's intentions or character?

Yes to all of the above.

The result can be feelings of disappointment, frustration, and discouragement. The challenges of life, however, can also be important learning experiences, and actually provide a step *forward* toward a goal.

My father was an immigration officer for decades—I understood his work and had watched it firsthand, spending a portion of my growing-up years with him as he interviewed people in Mexico for immigration sponsorship to the United States. I understood the value of other cultures. I respected people of other traditions.

Add to that the facts that I knew the products and services my business was promoting … I knew how to communicate on large stages before thousands, and also before small groups in living rooms … I knew how to travel and wasn't opposed to travel … and I knew the international business opportunity set before me was a great match for me! I threw myself into the adventure.

Not long ago I read a statement that described business as a "bumpy, scary, no-road-map thrill." That certainly was true for me! While I may not have had a *road map*, per se, I did not go into areas without contacts or a venue. And the adventure was certainly less "scary" because I was part of a bigger team. Nevertheless there were bumps and unknowns.

I recall one situation in which a man assured me repeatedly that he had a large number of people coming to see me and hear about the business opportunity I offered, and he had rented a fairly large room in which my presentation would be given. I arrived as planned and this man and I were the only people in attendance that night! It was a waste of my time, effort, and money to go there. ... Or was it?

I had discovered many years before that *nothing* is wasted when it is done "as unto the Lord." (See Colossians 3:23–24.)

I knew in this case that I had gone in good faith, seeking to *help* others help themselves toward a better life. I had done all the preparation for the event that I knew to do, and had also done all of the pre-screening of this man that I knew to do. While I could see no results as I left town the next day, I chose to believe that God might *still* be at work on those results! (Even now!)

I have also felt that way in other nations. The prospects seemed very positive and the people setting up my presentation meetings seemed not only genuine, but highly motivated and enthusiastic. The attendance, however, was poor and few people registered interest in continuing a business relationship.

In other cases, the initial meetings were highly successful and many people "signed on" to the opportunity offered to them ... and for a variety of reasons, some of which are still not fully known, the initial business group fizzled over the next year or two.

In a few cases, the people who seemed to be filled with integrity and honesty initially turned out to have much less integrity and very little concept of honesty as the income began flowing and the business began to build.

All in all, however, there were more successes than failures.

And that one fact—more successes than failures—can keep a business going, and growing.

I have told my colleagues repeatedly through the years, "You never know who is going to show up at a presentation that is presently only a date on your calendar. You do not know which meeting is going to have a real go-getter leader attending your presentation and hearing about your business for the first time. There is always the possibility of a real *winner* in your audience. Speak to that person with confidence and enthusiasm. In so doing, you will be speaking to the entire audience with confidence and enthusiasm. Win that one person in a way that is truly going to be beneficial and life-changing for that person, and you will be doing all that you can do, and all that you are required by God to do.

Lessons Learned on the International Stage

I went to Hungary shortly after the Berlin Wall was removed and West Germany and East Germany were in the beginning stages of reunification. I arrived in Budapest however, to discover that the "start-up" kits I had ordered for my meetings there had not been delivered in sufficient quantity, and the materials that had been delivered, were not collated and ready for distribution.

The man in charge of setting up my meeting went to the local military officials and hired a group of men to collate the kits—all several thousand of those kits were ready by dawn!

The lesson I learned: If you are going to get something done in another nation, seek out people with a reputation and experience in getting things done!

In Budapest. In Budapest, we made contact with a well-known woman who had grown up in Budapest and had become fairly famous as an actress in the United States. She traveled with us and was determined to help translate my business presentation. I had already hired a translator who had been recommended to me as someone who would translate accurately and fully *precisely* what I said, without any additions or deletions. I must admit, I had no confidence that this woman would do that ... and, as it turned out, she didn't. She had a message that *she* wanted to give. She began to argue with the interpreter. I had to be the referee. I knew that I wasn't offending anybody in the room, because nobody in the room understood English except this woman and the interpreter.

If anything, they would have concluded that I was in charge and had the ability to restore order to the meeting.

Later in the same trip, this woman told me that she had arranged an event at the country home of a friend for me to meet people and present information about my business. We headed off into the night, and trust me on this, it was a pitch-black night as we drove on country roads that seemed to have no markings whatsoever about where you were, or where the edge of the road might be.

We arrived at the meeting site that had only a tiny chalkboard and a tiny piece of chalk. She took over that meeting to tell her stories. I didn't understand, of course, what she was saying, but it seemed obvious that she was entertaining them with her stories. Nobody asked anything about my business. I chalked it up to an experience, but hardly a business meeting.

And there was still more. I went with her and her husband to a third appointment late one night. There were only a few people there. She announced at the end of the meeting that she and her husband were staying in the countryside, and that I should return to Budapest with the driver of the car I had hired. I began to pray in earnest. I didn't know this driver. I didn't speak his language and he didn't speak mine. I had no idea how far we were from my hotel in Budapest. I was in a total "trust God" position.

I was extremely grateful as you might imagine when I began to see the lights of Budapest and we pulled up in front of my hotel.

Why am I sharing this with you?

Very often, not only in your business, but in your *life*, you are going to encounter situations that may not be as serious as these were to me, but are nonetheless disconcerting and troublesome.

The four great lessons I learned were that a person ...

- *Must take control of the PURPOSE of a meeting or appointment.* If you have paid to travel to the meeting and have paid for the venue, and have a message you have been asked to give ... then you are in charge and at times, you must make that very clear to others who want to hijack your event.
- *Must get as much information as you can in advance of taking "detours" from an agreed-upon itinerary for a series of events or meetings.*
- *Must trust the Lord AT ALL TIMES when it comes to your protection.* God will use what you give to Him, in terms of your time, effort, talent, and resources. But He also wants you to trust Him for all the outcomes. He alone can protect you from *all evil.*

He alone can produce positive results from even the most negative situations or environments.

- *Travel with your own chalk and a marker that won't leak ink.*

In Greece. In Greece, we could not do any of our business presentations in one major city until we had a Greek Orthodox priest come and "bless" our event. We waited two hours for this man to arrive. We had a large bowl of water with a designated variety of green leaves ready for him according to his instructions. And it was only after he had spent a few minutes of "blessing" that we could proceed.

The lesson I learned: Know in advance what the local customs may be for "allowing" your meeting to begin, and work your schedule to allow for those customs to be fulfilled before the starting time of your first meeting.

In Eastern Europe. I once went to a beauty shop in an eastern European nation to have my hair cut and styled before a speaking event. The beauty operator took me into a back room where she turned on a gas pipe that suddenly shot out a flame. The procedure was for the woman to put a "curling iron," of sorts, into the flame and heat it up, and then use it on my wet hair both to dry and curl my hair. The smell of singed hair filled that room. I said, "Ma'am, I think I'll just let my hair dry naturally today."

At least I had a haircut.

The lesson I learned: Don't be afraid to change your course when you see things are not likely to end up in the way you desire!

In Romania. Romania was a difficult place to launch a business. We were in the capital city in the shadows of the government offices. The meeting was scheduled in an old building on the second floor. My team of about ten men and I began to walk up the staircase when suddenly, an older woman ahead of us fell. She tumbled all the way to the bottom of the stairs and there she lay. Dead.

Nobody had touched her. Nobody moved to help her. The men with me told me that we just needed to move on. Apparently everybody else in the hotel lobby was of the same mind. The man who was closest to me said, "There is nobody to help her. She is dead. Eventually somebody will move her body."

I couldn't stand that! I insisted that she be carried to a private area, where somebody could truly examine her to make certain she was dead. My team arranged that, and indeed, she had died.

I once had a man go with me on a trip to help me set up meetings to promote our business. He took ten men to help him with the meeting. I discovered one evening that he had hired six Greek girls to help him and his staff sort the applications that had been submitted during the meeting. I smelled something fishy. It was midnight! He needed six beautiful young girls to help ten men sort paperwork? I confronted him and told him to shut down these shenanigans. If I and one assistant could provide all the follow-up necessary for the response from *my* meeting, and I was higher on the totem pole than this man, surely he and *ten* men could process the responses from *his* meeting.

The lesson I learned: Maintain your nose for detecting "fishy" circumstances or statements!

In Turkey. I had some interesting—even scary—experiences in Turkey. I was evacuated from one evening session, along with others on my overall business team, because of a bomb scare that had been phoned into the venue. We scattered as quickly as we could, along with the 5,000 people in attendance.

On one occasion, I was invited to meet a very prominent businessman in another city. My two business partners and I had dinner with this man who had four body guards waiting by his Mercedes limo. He proceeded to pick up food with his hands and tried to put it in my mouth. He told my associates that business was over and he was taking me home to be his wife. I have rarely been as scared as I was that evening.

I told the men who had arranged the meeting that I wanted them to call a cab for me *immediately* and that they were not to leave me alone with this man for one second. These associates had never seen me angry before, but they saw me angry that night!

At this time, I was traveling solo, setting up business meetings and conducting them on my own. When the prophecy came that I would no longer be traveling by myself overseas, but would travel as part of a team, you can only imagine how I rejoiced.

The lesson I learned: Whenever possible, do NOT travel alone!

Some Lessons Involved Humor. Not all of my "lessons learned" in trusting the Lord have been intense or moderately dangerous. Some have had a funny side.

On one trip my son Paul was with me and we ordered room service at the hotel where we were staying. We ordered "sausage and eggs" from the menu and both of us laughed heartily when the sausage showed up as Vienna sausages and the eggs were runny. We were grateful that there was a McDonald's just down the street! We rarely ate at McDonald's in the USA, but we were grateful for that chain overseas because we could always rely on clean facilities and familiar food.

The lesson I learned: Travel with a "hot pot." A hot pot enabled me to heat up water for coffee or tea, and sometimes for the making of instant oatmeal or ramen-style noodle soup or instant soup packets.

Three General Lessons that Were Always Important. Regardless of circumstances, I learned that my business travels were not *only* for *business*. They were part of God's faith journey for me. Once I became acutely aware of that truth, I began to spend lots of nighttime flights in prayer, trusting God to bring the right people to the meetings I was scheduled to hold the next day.

I also learned that I needed to send a strong message *very early in a relationship* that I was not at all interested in working with people who were deceptive, manipulative, or dishonest. I only wanted to work with people of integrity and honesty. The message usually went out early, "Don't mess with Beverly."

Finally, I learned to send a message in advance of a meeting, if possible, that I was in strong favor of building good businesses that would help families stay together in strength, and provide good help for their children and eventually, their grandchildren, as well as their neighbors and ultimately, their nation as a whole.

How did these decisions reflect faith?

First, I went into every meeting, and every nation, looking for what God might want to do in me, or through me.

Second, I went into every event and appointment with my character intact, fully expecting that others would deal with me as honorably as I intended to deal with them.

Third, I went into new opportunities seeking to produce win-win results, not only in business, but in friendship and faith.

I am fully convinced that God desires to use *all* things in our lives to bring Him honor, and that He fully desires to bless people of all nations, races, and cultures. We are His agents and the vessels for pouring out His love. We must be mindful of that at all times.

7

Escaping the Deadly Traps

There are some situations in life that *feel* like deadly traps—they might not actually kill you, but they can kill or destroy an aspect of your life and may slow you down to the state of near paralysis. These traps may start out in one realm of life, such as business or health, but they eventually become a "spiritual issue." And, it is in the spiritual realm that a person often finds relief or rescue from the deadly trap!

I once felt miserably trapped in a business relationship that I had entered without checking out all aspects of the relationship. I was devastated by the accusations hurled at me, and by the actions taken against me. Sadly I didn't seek God's wisdom. The mistake impacted my life, my current income, my future income, my children, and every area of my life. I sought counseling with this business partner to attempt some form of reconciliation. Repeatedly, I was led to a conclusion on the part of the counselor that I must be the person who was one hundred percent at fault. Make sure you have the right advice.

At one very low point when a specific committee convened to confront me, I took a quick look at the group gathered and knew immediately that each person in the room was under the influence of one man who had set me up to take the fall and "be" the enemy. I was the only woman in the room, by the way. The man "behind the screen" of this confrontation was well-liked by other men in the organization in which we both worked, and he was perceived to be a person of good character with the power to destroy competitors or those who opposed him. The people who had been influenced by this man were definitely duped on the first assessment (his character), and in my opinion, greatly overestimated his influence or ability to control.

Nevertheless, business is sometimes a matter of perception more than reality. That isn't fair, it isn't right, but it often *is*. A person is never wise to say, "I don't care *at all* what others think of me or say about me." I have made it a point in my life to care *MOST* of all what God thinks about me, and secondly, what my family members and mentors think about me. But that isn't to say that I have *no* regard for what my business associates, customers, or new recruits think of me. Their opinions do matter, and I take it as a personal responsibility to make sure that opinions about me are based on solid evidence—facts and situations that are irrefutable and solid.

Did I have any idea I was being set up?

No. I was told we were having a "board meeting" related to our company.

I was devastated by the accusations brought against me. I refused to retaliate by telling things I knew about various ones in the room—the only outcome of that would have been further division and very possibly the destruction of a few marriages.

The man at the center of the opposition against me had said to me on more than one occasion, "If I go down, you go down." He had made it known to others who worked under him, "If I go down, you all go down." There were millions of dollars at stake and this man was so intent on winning, he was willing to put all that he had and all that others under him had earned or developed at risk. He was going to take others with him into the losing column without any regard to personal loyalty or equanimity.

What happened? The dispute went to the highest legal authorities for our type of business. The top legal counselor confronted the man who was at the center of this mess with the fact that he was destroying his own business out of vengeance, hatred, and spite. I quietly made moves to have the people who worked with me and were loyal to me *join* me in my international lines of business.

Did anybody in that original confrontation ever admit he was mistaken or ask for my forgiveness? No. More than two decades have passed. My business has grown. For this I only can praise God.

In the months that followed, I carefully considered an opportunity to begin a new business in Australia. And then, I was approached by my friends Jim and Nancy to join them in a venture that was based in Atlanta. I took them up on their proposal and as I once heard it said, "the future began to be launched."

I initially told a wise business counselor, "I can't stand up to this pressure. I can't stand up to the hatred and lies." He responded, "One woman probably can't. But one woman *with GOD* can."

That statement went to the very core of my heart. I knew he was right and that my life was not to be based upon what other people did or didn't do, but rather, on what God called me to do and the way in which I would respond to that call with faith.

A Jealous Spirit Is a Difficult Foe. Throughout my life I have had to deal with a number of people who developed a jealous spirit toward me. They resented what I had—usually without any understanding about how much time and effort I had spent to achieve what I had achieved. These people never *talked* to me directly about why I have chosen to do what I do. Nor did they ever investigate or consider how I was truly *using* my talents and *expressing* my values in my business.

I could have spent many months' worth of time—years, perhaps, of time—in trying to justify myself to my critics. I chose to remain silent and move forward and upward. I was reminded early in my musical career that those who resented my success as a musician or conductor seemed to believe they would elevate their own standing in the music community if they could put me down a notch. They failed to see that life doesn't truly work that way—certainly not in the long run. Their words of criticism lingered in the air about as long as the newspaper or newsletter in which they voiced their criticism stayed on the newsstand. In other words, written today and in the trash tomorrow.

The New Testament tells a story that came to my mind frequently when I heard about the criticism of someone. In this incident, the apostle Peter was invited to go to the house of a Gentile. Peter was a godly Jew and to visit the home of a Gentile was virtually unheard of. He knew he would receive a great deal of criticism from other Jews if he accepted the invitation. He was troubled about what to do. The Lord showed him in a vision that all people have value in God's eyes. It was not up to Peter to make a decision about who had value and who didn't.

He was to go where he was made welcome and not worry about his critics.

I adopted that same attitude. I intentionally and consciously—and *repeatedly*—made a decision that I would work with the people who wanted to work with me, perform for the people who invited me to perform for them, and enjoy my life. I knew my values and my reasons. I knew when I performed well and when I may have had an "off" night. I didn't need a "critic" to make me humble or to educate me about my faults—whether on the musical stage or in my business presentations.

I also came to this conclusion: All work has value. God has an amazing way of using everything we do if we seek to honor Him in our work and to work with humility, fairness, diligence, and the best quality we can produce.

And finally, I also concluded that there simply is no such thing as "constructive criticism." There is constructive mentoring and teaching—but this is always within the *relationship* that a person has with a mentor, about whom there is no question when it comes to their loyalty and love. Criticism from strangers or distant acquaintances is not constructive, and in most cases, it is rooted in a desire to destroy or harm, not a desire to encourage, show love, or produce good.

These principles have stood the test of time for me. Those who criticized me years ago … well, frankly, I have difficulty remembering their names. What they said didn't change me or deter me. I didn't use any anger I could have felt toward them to fuel my motivation—I chose to draw inspiration and motivation from *positive* sources, from the encouragement I received from my mentors, and from experiences that were loaded with beauty, meaning, and spiritual refreshment. In the end, my critics did not produce anything of quality in my life, or in the lives of those with whom I worked or to whom I spoke.

If I had any concern whatsoever with what people were saying about me behind my back, or writing about me, I made that concern a matter of prayer. Like Peter in the Bible story, I gave the consequences of their criticism to God and said, "Here. I'm giving this person to You. I trust You to deal with them in Your wisdom and love. Free me from their negative influence. Give me the desire and courage to forgive them and to release them from my mind and heart. Help me to trust You and You alone with my current circumstances and the future You have already designed for me."

If you have never prayed a prayer like that, I encourage you to read through that prayer again. God has something better for you than discouragement and despair related to those who might mistreat or abuse you, including those who mistreat and abuse through words of criticism.

Very often criticism is a "polite" word that is wrapped around a kernel of hatred, prejudice, resentment, or bitterness. Wake up and recognize that your harshest critic is likely jealous of you, or dislikes you because you are succeeding in a way that he or she desires but isn't willing to work for. Pray that this person will be able to let go of their hate, resentment, bitterness, or prejudice, and to turn the energy they have devoted to those negative emotions into productive, positive words and deeds. Only then will they begin to grow as a person.

Trusting God

At times in life there is simply no good recourse other than to say, "I trust You, God!" The need to trust God is a huge realization for any woman, or man, to have. I hope that you never have to go through an experience of betrayal and false accusations, but if you do, I trust that you will turn to God for your strength and *TRUST HIM!* Listen closely to what He advises you to do, and obey Him—even if it is contrary to the way you feel or what you want to do out of a sense of vengeance or self-justification.

God's Word says that

- God can turn *all* things to your good. (See Romans 8:28.)
- We are to leave all matters of revenge or vengeance to the Lord. (See Romans 2:19.)

Dealing with Abuse

Trust in God is vital in two areas of life that are quite common to women worldwide: abuse and authority. Abuse is inevitably an issue of power. Authority inevitably involves issues of submission and leadership.

One thing I've learned with certainty is that countless women live in an atmosphere of violence. They are ritualistically abused verbally, physically, and sometimes sexually by their own husbands or another adult male in the household. They live in fear, never knowing when the next attack is going to come their way. They are afraid to speak up, and they are also afraid to leave—they fear that nobody will believe "their side" of a story and that the persecution they will face in the wake of that experience will be even worse than what they have experienced before.

Even pastors' wives suffer from abuse. We must never discount the extent of evil in our world today. It happens in every profession and economic situation. No one looking at me would have guessed the amount of abuse to which I was subjected.

I *never* encourage a woman to stay in an abusive situation, and especially never to stay if she senses that her children are in danger or are being consistently abused verbally, physically, or sexually. She needs to flee … and to flee sooner rather than later. There are many shelters and "safe places" where women can go and be helped. She needs to run to one of those places and allow herself and her children to heal and then be helped to make a new life that is safe and healthy. "Divorce" is not the real issue in these cases. "Safety" is. God doesn't like divorce, but God REALLY doesn't like abuse.

When children see their mother being abused by their father, they begin to fear their mother as well as their father. They see their mother as being a "participant" in her own abuse, even if that is not the way the mother feels or intends. From the child's point of view, a mother who stays in abuse is sending a signal that abuse is an acceptable way to live.

Abuse is a "power play" on the part of a person to control another person. It is using another person as a whipping post for venting his own anger, bitterness, or hatred. Abuse is often totally disassociated with a victim's words or deeds. A person who lived for many years on the big island in Hawaii once said, "Abuse is a volcano that can erupt at any time. The land around the volcano does not cause the eruption. The volcano erupts when it wants to, with a power that nobody and nothing outside the volcano can predict or control." That is the way abuse functions.

There are times when women are spoken to in a way that is disrespectful. There are also times when a man may vent his anger—not at his wife specifically but in a general way toward life, making harsh and abrasive statements. If a woman is spoken to with disrespect, she must respect *herself* enough to say, "You will not speak that way to me. I am not your verbal punching bag and I will not be an audience of one to your hateful and angry opinions. I am walking out of this room and when you are ready to speak in a kind and respectful tone of voice, I will be available to you. Until then, stay away."

You may ask, "But does a woman really have that authority or power?"

Yes, she does. And if the man does not respect her statement and keep his distance, she needs to put even more distance between herself and her husband, and take her children with her.

In many homes around the world, it is the woman who sets the emotional boundaries of the home—including what the children say, as well as what their husbands say. Most men do not want to be estranged from their wives or children … they do not want to be "alone" in life and they do not want people outside the home to suspect that they cannot control their anger or their verbiage. Women have much more authority in this area than they often think they have.

At the same time, women must take responsibility for their own anger and verbiage. They must not threaten their husbands idly, or be abusive to their husbands. They must learn to deal with their personal anger and frustrations in a way that is healthy—never taking out their anger or bitterness on their husbands or children.

In simple practical terms, sometimes the best thing a woman can do is to "break the moment." That can be as simple as leaving the house and going to a place of safety.

A woman needs to give herself time to catch her breath and to step back and look at her situation as objectively as possible.

There are other things that may help, and at bare minimum, help a woman prepare herself for appointments with counselors or law-enforcement officials. One of those things is to write down feelings and details of incidents in a journal. There is very little benefit in voicing complaints or making demands if your emotions are at a fever pitch. Let things calm down. Choose to see your situation—or the specific argument or issue—as objectively and rationally as possible.

Blair Singer said, "When your emotions go high, your intelligence goes down."

Look for God's wisdom. Get God's solution. Pray and wait for God to reveal His plan and His timing.

Facing an Accusation of "Unsubmissive." For years, I was accused by a few well-meaning men for having brought some problems on myself because I hadn't been "submissive" to my husband. There is a very bad understanding in the world, and especially in the church circles, it seems, when it comes to the word *submissive*. To be submissive means to "yield"—and yielding happens in the context of decisions, usually about matters that are not life-and-death or eternal in nature, but rather, matters of style and procedure. The submissive person says, "I am willing to yield a particular decision to *you*. I give you the authority to make the choice, with full awareness that you are then *responsible* for the choice that you make." Those who take on authority *always* take on a responsibility for what they have chosen to "rule over"! That's the Bible's rule of reciprocity. If you have authority, you have responsibility.

The Bible tells us that we are to be submissive *one* to another *in the body of Christ*. We are to yield to one another on matters of style and procedure rather than fight about these things that cause great dissension that distract us from the more important things in life—the raising up of children who are godly and good citizens, the establishment of ministries and outreaches that win people to the Lord and develop the faith of believers, and so forth.

Submission never means lying down and being a doormat for another person to walk upon. And, it is never a justifiable excuse for a person to sin. I know of at least three men right now who are justifying their adulterous relationships on the basis of "my wife wasn't submissive." Oh really? Those men need to read the Bible's full statement about submission. It says that husbands are to *love* their wives in a self-sacrificial way, just as Christ loved the church. In that context and in that emotional atmosphere, wives are to yield or submit to their husbands. Let me assure you, I have not met many wives who were *unwilling* to yield to husbands who were generous, self-sacrificing, and loving!

In many cases where a woman is accused of being "unsubmissive," the flip side of that relationship is a husband who is selfish, stingy, and unloving. There is little a wife can do except pray that God will move on the heart of the husband. When selfishness is involved—either on the part of the man or woman—a dispute seems inevitable. A good relationship of any kind involves a huge amount of giving ... of listening, or waiting, or exhibiting kindness and mercy.

Asking Others for Help. In later years at various times I sought counsel to solve relationship issues. If the other party or parties are not willing to cooperate it is futile.

Avoiding the Traps

As much as possible, of course, a woman will want to try to AVOID the deadly emotional traps that seek to destroy her reputation, integrity, and peace of mind and heart. I encourage women everywhere to be very cautious if they encounter people who are:

- *Abusers.* These are people who try to "out-power" you ... to purposefully hurt you in order to advance their own positions.
- *Wasters.* These are people who waste your time, use what they can of your resources, or waste your energy in unproductive activities or meetings.
- *Hangers on.* These are people who try to gain greater fame or acceptance by hanging on to your coattails and using your reputation to give them entrée into a meeting or inner circle of some type.

Be wary of these people. In the long run, they are not your friends and they do not make good business partners. Not ever, no matter how wealthy or influential they may appear to be.

God's Word Can Give You Strength

I have learned to go to God's Word when I need inner strength. Here are several verses that always build up my faith to trust God for total deliverance and the best possible outcome:

Isaiah 41:10

Fear not, for I am with you;
Be not dismayed, for I am your God.
I will strengthen you.
Yes, I will help you.
I will uphold you with my righteous right hand.

1 Peter 4:12–13 (NASB)

Beloved, do not be surprised at the fiery ordeal among you, which comes upon you for your testing, as though some strange thing were happening to you; but to the degree that you share the sufferings of Christ, keep on rejoicing, so that also at the revelation of His glory you may rejoice with exultation.

Psalm 103:1–5 (NASB)

Bless the LORD, O my soul, and all that is within me, bless His holy name. Bless the LORD, O my soul, and forget none of His benefits; who pardons all your iniquities, Who heals all your diseases; Who redeems your life from the pit, Who crowns you with lovingkindness and compassion; Who satisfies your years with good things, so that your youth is renewed like the eagle.

Psalm 51:12–13 (NASB)

Restore to me the joy of Your salvation and sustain me with a willing spirit. Then I will teach transgressors Your ways and sinners will be converted to You.

2 Corinthians 4:7–10 (NASB)

But we have this treasure in earthen vessels, so that the surpassing greatness of the power will be of God and not from ourselves; we are afflicted in every way, but not crushed; perplexed, but not despairing; persecuted, but not forsaken, struck down, but not destroyed; always carrying about in the body the dying of Jesus, so that the life of Jesus also may be manifested in our body.

8

A Wellspring of Encouragement

D own through the years God has sent a number of people into my life at precise times for precise purposes. I knew they were God-sent. I listened to them, learned from them, and I gleaned from them ideas that I could use in my business and life.

I especially have drawn strength and encouragement from those who have told me *their* stories of tragedy or despair, and who came through those experiences with a stronger faith and an increased ability to empathize with others and be of service to them.

Not all of the people who have inspired me and encouraged me have been people I know personally, although I feel as if I know them. They are women who have written books or made DVD series that have greatly blessed me. Joyce Meyer and Beth Moore were very influential in showing me that a woman can not only live through abuse, but be a true overcomer and a strong encourager of other women who are in abusive relationships. I learned from Kay Arthur the importance of speaking always about what GOD can do. Each of these women encouraged me by their example to immerse myself in the Word of God, and not only to read it but *learn* it, and memorize it and sing it and speak it and LIVE it.

In this chapter I want to share with you from the wellspring of encouragement that I have gained from other women I *do* know personally. I trust their stories will bless and inspire you.

My Friend Diane

I don't know many people who have had a more difficult childhood than my friend Diane. She grew up primarily in the inner city. Her family was extremely poor and she was abused in almost every way possible.

Diane's parents divorced when she was three years old, and that was only the beginning of great instability that plagued much of her childhood and teenage years. She was moved from one family to the next, feeling unwanted wherever she found herself. The frequent moves meant that she changed schools almost yearly, so she had little sense of belonging in any neighborhood or school. She grew up with an abiding sense of being rejected and abandoned.

On one occasion, Diane came home from school to find that her mother had moved out of state! On another occasion, she recalls hiding with an aunt in the center of town, watching as the aunt's drunken husband drove up and down the streets with the intention of running over Diane and killing her.

On yet another occasion, Diane's mother put an ad in the newspaper for someone to take Diane off her hands. That turned out to be a terrible experience for her, filled with abuse.

Diane was sexually abused from the time she was four years old. She became hard and bitter as a result of all these horrors of her early childhood and eventually, she found it safer to live on the streets than with any type of "guardian" who might be assigned to her. She became heavily involved in drinking and using drugs.

And then she met a woman named Ruby.

Diane was living in St. Louis, Missouri, at the time, and Ruby seemed drawn to her and became a mother figure in her life. Diane was very resistant toward Ruby's love—she had been so badly wounded and it was almost beyond her to trust anyone. Even so, Ruby persisted in loving Diane.

Diane had a mental breakdown and was hospitalized. But Ruby was there.

She went through a roller-coaster time of emotional trauma related to substance use during her teen years. But Ruby stayed by her side.

Diane readily admits that in her extreme bitterness, she was not an easy person to love. But Ruby was like a mother bear with a cub. She simply would not give up on Diane.

When Ruby's husband made a decision to move the family back to their home state of Arkansas, Ruby informed Diane that she wasn't going to move unless Diane agreed to come with them. Diane agreed to go—not because she particularly wanted to go, but because she knew that Arkansas was where Ruby and her family belonged. Looking back, Diane thinks this may have been one of the first unselfish acts of her entire life, and it certainly turned out to be one of the most important decisions in Diane's life.

It was in Arkansas that Diane learned about salvation through Jesus Christ.

She told me one time, "My life was at the end of the road. I had no hope or future. My boyfriend's mother pressured my boyfriend to go to church, and he, in turn, persuaded me to go with him. I agreed because I figured I could also use some 'points' in case there was any chance at all of my making it into heaven some day. I had never really seen any value in going to church. My life was such a mess I had concluded long ago that God didn't love me and would never love me.

"But," she continued, "when I attended a revival service in that little country church in Arkansas, God's Spirit stirred within me. I didn't really understand what I was feeling inside. I asked my boyfriend to take me over to a mutual friend's house. Her name was Fran and she went to church about twice a year so I figured she'd probably know what was going on in me. I asked Fran to explain why I felt as if I had forty pounds of pressure right on my chest. I said to her, 'I feel as if I'm very close to finding something I've been looking for all my life … but I don't know what it is!'

"Fran told me about salvation and that Jesus Christ had died on the cross so that every person who believed in Him could be forgiven of their sins, have a personal relationship with God, and go to heaven one day. She explained that Jesus was a completely sinless man who had died in my place—He had paid my sin debt through His death on the cross.

"It was the first time I had ever heard the Gospel message of salvation through believing in Jesus. I said, 'Lord, if You want my life, I want You to take it, because I am sooo tired of living the way I've been living.' In my heart I truly believed in God Almighty, in Jesus Christ as God's Son, in the Holy Spirit, and that God had raised Jesus from the dead. I wanted the Holy Spirit to come into my life, heal me, and start my life over. I was entirely ready to give my life to God so I could live under His direction.

"I had a powerful spiritual experience that night. I knew the Holy Spirit had come to live within my spirit. I sensed the peace I had been looking for all my life, and I knew God had heard my prayer. My life was dramatically changed. And, I have served the Lord passionately ever since. I have been in ministry for most of my adult life, and I presently am a missionary with Cross Connection Ministries."

Diane's decision to receive Jesus as her Savior suddenly gave her a "family heritage." She became part of God's family! It also gave her a tremendous sense of security—her eternal destiny was certain and God's presence with her always could be counted on. She had a future and a hope, and a confidence that no matter where God, her spiritual Father, might send her, she would never be alone or rejected.

Diane began to read the Bible and to learn how to discern God's Spirit speaking deep within her. She began to trust Him for every decision she faced in her life. And she began sharing her story and her understanding about her loving Father with people wherever and whenever the opportunity arose. She describes her relationship with God as "the sweet fellowship between a Father and a child"—something Diane never knew in her physical childhood years, but something she continues to experience in her spiritual life.

I am always amazed when I hear stories like Diane's. I grew up in a church knowing about God's love ... and I wandered away from a steady obedience to God's plan for me. Diane grew up knowing nothing about God's love ... and then wandered into a setting where she heard and responded quickly to God's plan for her, and she has walked out that plan with steadfastness.

My Friend Florence

My dear friend and one of my foremost mentors, Florence Littauer, was born in Haverhill, Massachusetts, to a family that operated a small neighborhood corner store. The family lived above the store. As a child, Florence had one main ambition: to make enough money to move out of Haverhill. Her father encouraged her to go to college but her mother was more cautious. She advised her to get good grades and become an office secretary.

Florence received a scholarship to the University of Massachusetts when she finished high school. She earned a degree in English and later went back to college to get a certificate so she might teach speech and drama classes—she then taught English, speech, and drama classes at the high school level.

Florence grew up in a time when many young women aspired to get an education, get a good job, and marry a wealthy man. There certainly are a number of young women today who have that same three-fold goal in mind.

Florence met Fred at a summer camp where she was a counselor for young girls. She knew nothing about his family. After the summer was over, she and Fred continued to correspond and eventually, Fred invited her to come visit him at his family home in New York. She arrived to discover that Fred lived in a mansion. When the time came for dinner, Fred escorted his mother to the dining table, which was set with the finest of linens, china, sterling silver flatware, and crystal stemware. They enjoyed an elegant meal. The meal was served by a maid, and everything was done in a first-class manner. Florence couldn't help but think, "This is a long way from living over a corner store."

Florence was and is a very practical woman and she admitted to me that security and a fine life were far more important to her initially than being "in love," although she certainly loved Fred. She asked rhetorically, "Would you rather marry a man with whom you are madly in love—a young good-looking guy who has no goals, no education, and no job, or marry a man who has goals, an education, and a job, and who is acceptable in appearance, even though you are not head-over-heels in love?" For Florence, the answer was the latter.

She knew that Fred was ambitious and that he would do well at whatever he pursued. After they married, they moved several times as he advanced his way upward in a food-service position with a large restaurant chain.

In the next few years Florence gave birth to two darling girls a couple of years apart. Later she gave birth to a baby boy who had serious birth defects. He died when he was just six months old. Florence and Fred were both devastated but their doctor encouraged them to try again for a baby, assuring them that this kind of defect wouldn't happen again. But it did. Florence again gave birth to a baby boy and he died of the same deformities. Several years later, they adopted a baby boy and named him Fred. These years were a time of great struggle for Florence, and also for Fred and for their marriage. Many couples find that the death of a child destroys their husband-wife relationship, and especially if an inherited illness or deformity might be involved in the child's death. Florence and Fred had gone through this tragedy not just once, but twice, in a short period of time.

It was during this time that they were introduced to Christ Jesus and they made a decision to receive Him as their Savior and then follow Him wherever He might lead them. They began to study the Bible and they found in their relationship with Christ and their Bible studies the help and strength they needed to go forward in their lives.

They soon began to lead Bible studies. Even though they were far from experts in the Christian life, they were good communicators, very transparent about their experience, and totally devoted to the Lord. They were young and had what many considered to be a "fresh testimony" and their Bible studies grew in popularity.

When their adopted son was about three years old, Fred and Florence moved to California where Fred was given the job of heading up a large food-service operation for a non-profit organization. The days were busy for Fred, and lonely for Florence. They had moved to a small bungalow in California, and Florence missed both the big house of their early marriage years and her teaching responsibilities.

She set out to make friends in her new community, and soon, people were inviting her to speak to their neighborhood group or church group. She was highly appreciated as a gifted communicator—very humorous, but also capable of giving challenging messages embedded with profound truths. She became quite popular as a speaker.

One day Florence read a book on personality types. She felt as if her eyes were suddenly opened as to just how different she and Fred were! They embarked together on a quest to improve their marriage, and to gain understanding about how people of very different personalities might complement and complete each other. Eventually they left the non-profit organization where Fred was employed and had a speaking ministry together. They also wrote books together.

Florence was quick to point out to me that she spoke for more than ten years for *free* before she was ever paid for any speaking engagement.

In the end, the books that Fred and Florence wrote together were translated into many languages and millions of people read them and were helped by their honest and simple explanations about how people can get along and accomplish great tasks, even if they have different personality types.

I met Florence and Fred during a very difficult emotional time in my life, and they ministered to me personally in a wonderful and powerful way. After Fred died, Florence and I remained friends. I admired the way she continued to live the life God had set before her even though her husband was no longer by her side on stage or at her writing desk.

Part of my message to women around the world has been drawn from what I observed in Florence's life. I see in Florence a woman whom God has used because she kept her spirit humble before Him. She allowed God to use her difficulties to show His love and mercy.

I have admired Florence for the compassion she feels for people in all stations of life. She knows that many people look "great" on the outside, but on the inside, they are crying and in pain. She never embarrasses another person, but she does reach out to them in a way that allows them to know that she fully understands the depth of their emotions and sorrow. Her message is always that God has a purpose for all things, and that He can heal a woman's heart and use her to accomplish great things that she has not even imagined.

Florence is one of several women that God has used to speak to me a message that the Lord seems to repeat again and again through my life: "God knows. God loves. God heals and helps. And God has a purpose for you to take His love, healing, and help to others."

GOD KNOWS. He knows precisely where you are and what you are going through. He already knows the way *through* your difficulty. He has already planned the good results that lie ahead!

GOD LOVES. No matter what the circumstances, or even the enormity of a particular sin, God loves. It is His nature. He confronts us with His love and says, "I forgive. Go forward in your life and don't sin in that way again." God does not punish us, but rather, leads us with His love to see beyond our past and into the future that He desires for us.

GOD HEALS AND HELPS. God is always at work to bring us to greater wholeness—in spirit, mind, emotions, body, relationships, and material blessings. He desires to help us every day to make the right decisions and choices, and to set the right goals. He helps us by sending us the right opportunities, and the right people to work alongside.

GOD'S PURPOSE IS ALWAYS IN EFFECT. God never loses interest in us or sets us on a shelf. He never disqualifies us from living out the plan He has designed for us. His primary goal is that we live in a way that becomes a living portrait of His love, His healing power, and His divine purpose to forgive and bless.

My Friend Else

My friend Else in Denmark was raised in a home that had grown "cold" toward the Lord. Her older siblings were all taken to Sunday school at the Lutheran church her parents attended. But Else and her younger sister rarely went to church. Part of the reason was this: Before Else was born, her mother had given birth to a son, who died when he was only two years old. Else later realized that her mother had become greatly discouraged in her faith after the little boy died. Even so, Else told me one time that her mother had been the foremost person to teach her about forgiveness, and that it was important to smile instead of cry.

When she was only eleven years old, Else ended up in a hospital where physicians diagnosed her with a heart disease. The medical world was just learning how to treat her particular ailment—a few years earlier and physicians may not have been able to do the procedures that saved her life. Even though she came through the operations successfully, doctors told her that she should never attempt to have a child—the strain would be too great on her heart. When she was in her early twenties, however, doctors gave her permission to try for a pregnancy and shortly after that, she did become pregnant and gave birth to a son. She knew without anybody preaching a sermon to her that God can and does heal, and that miracles are possible.

As the daughter of Lutheran parents, Else had been baptized in the church as an infant cradled in her godmother's arms. At fourteen, she had gone through confirmation classes. During these classes, the priest at the Lutheran church taught her about faith and God's unconditional love. She emerged from those classes with a strong belief that God had a plan for her life and that everything in life happens for a reason.

It was this understanding about God and faith that carried Else through her heart surgeries and other experiences in her life in which she came very close to death. Each time the medical world managed to "rescue" her, she saw the incident as one more example that God still had a plan for her.

Her near-death experiences also gave her a deep sense of gratitude for each new day, which she believed was a gift from God to her. She has lived her life with a strong sense of responsibility for being the best she can be in all things, and getting the most out of every experience set before her. Her motivation is to help as many people as she can to love God, love themselves, and love other people.

Every person has a unique "faith journey"—a path that leads them to God, and a path that God then leads them to walk all the way through life to eternity!

My Friend Renee

My friend Renee accepted Jesus when she was only four years old! She responded to an invitation given by the pastor at her church to come to the altar of the church and receive Jesus as her Savior. It was a day that she still remembers, and it was a decision that shaped the rest of her childhood and early teen years.

Then, as a teenager, Renee allowed her own lack of self-esteem to push her into a dating relationship at a young age, and she later ran away with a young man who had convinced her that he was the only one who would ever want to marry her. Renee struggled with not feeling pretty enough or smart enough to achieve much in life, even though she is a lovely woman who has plenty of brain power!

Immediately after she married, she knew she had made a huge mistake. She had been taught, however, that divorce was wrong and remarriage after a divorce was even "more wrong," so she was determined to stay in the bad marriage and "make it work." She did, for nine years. Her husband came and went from the marriage, but Renee was determined to follow the Lord and raise her son according to God's Word, in spite of her own misery.

When her husband finally left "for good" and the divorce happened, Renee had a strong feeling of assurance in her heart that God would be with her as she recovered from the divorce. During her marriage, she had experienced recurring bouts of depression, and those who knew her during her marriage and saw her after the divorce could hardly believe the difference in her countenance. She no longer "looked" depressed! She no longer felt a pervasive feeling of suffering.

Renee told the Lord at the time of the divorce, "If You let me escape from this mistake of my own making, I will be content to be alone." And she has been.

I in no way believe that a person who is divorced needs to stay unmarried, but I also know that if that is how God leads a person, the woman can be very content in her life and feel satisfied and fulfilled. Renee is a tremendous example of this to me.

Renee has a very responsible position in the business world today. She had a dream about the job a full two years before it was offered to her. She dreamed that she was living in another city and was attending a church there. It was a church she had attended in the past on a few occasions so she recognized it. This dream opened her heart and mind to the idea of taking a risk and moving to that city. It was a bold move for her because it meant moving away from her family, who had been helping her as she raised her son.

Then a call came for a job interview. In her words, the call was "out of the blue." The dream had led her to be receptive to the idea of the move, and then the idea of the job. She accepted the position offered to her.

The job has included a great deal of international travel, and great financial responsibilities for a very large and complicated corporation. She is succeeding in all ways!

Beyond the challenges of her job, Renee has been through health trials—including cancer, a serious eye condition, and also other relationship and career difficulties. But, in her words, "The Lord has been with me through each one, and each experience has built my faith." One of the areas in which she has relied greatly upon God has been "discernment." She told me, "Each job along my career path has prepared me for the next. I have had a growing understanding about discernment. I have encountered instances when people lied to me very boldly and with such confidence that I needed the wisdom of God to discern the truth and to sort out a situation and take the right actions. There have also been instances when I was traveling and I needed to discern the evil that was nearby—and then trust God to protect me from it. In all of the challenges that have come my way, I have grown to have an abiding sense that God cares about even my most insignificant need."

Renee is strong in prayer, strong in reading God's Word, and has a wonderful sense of gratitude for God's work in her life.

My Friend Tina

Not many years ago, I met a young woman at church named Tina. She had a story that left me amazed at God's sovereign ways and tenderness toward each person.

When Tina was only three months old, her mother abandoned their home. Her father was in the military and was an alcoholic. His parents—her grandparents—were also alcoholics, but they banded together to raise Tina as best they could. She remembers much of her childhood as being spent in bars while her grandparents and dad drank and talked with their friends. They'd buy her a nonalcoholic Shirley Temple drink and taught her how to play cards and shoot pool.

Then her father remarried and she suddenly had step-sisters and step-brothers. She began to use drugs, and when she was a teenager, her stepmother kicked her out of the house. She went to live with a friend, and got her first job at a fast-food restaurant.

Tina married at age nineteen and she and her husband Josh moved out of state. They both drank heavily. Tina had given birth to a little girl when she was single, and after she and Josh married, he adopted the little girl.

It was Tina's little girl who first got her to attend an evangelical church, and to continue to attend it. Her daughter was only five years old at the time, but she was adamant that Tina needed to go to church with her, and she wouldn't take "no" for an answer!

Tina and Josh had a son together after they married. One day when the little boy was three Tina was drinking at the neighbor's house. He came running in the door of their neighbor's house and put his hands on her cheeks and said, "Mom, what are you *doing*?" She didn't understand the fullness of his question, but later, she did enter a twelve-step program to get help for what everybody around her knew—including her three-year-old son. She had a serious alcohol addiction.

Tina and Josh eventually divorced and went their separate ways. Their son stayed with Tina, and by the time of their separation, her daughter had grown up and moved out on her own. Tina and Josh were apart for about a year and then they got back together and entered counseling to see if there was any hope for them as a couple. They ultimately remarried, and this time, their marriage was far more healthy.

They are both sober and have been sober for a good length of time now. Josh has a good job and so does Tina. Their daughter is now a Marine, as is her husband.

My Friend Jules

My friend Jules did not grow up with deep spiritual roots. She did not attend a church regularly as a girl. She described the situation to me one time in this way: "There were several times I stumbled into church alongside my great grandmother, grandmother, cousin, or even a school friend. We mostly went to weddings and funerals."

She does remember, however, that as a child, she periodically "shot prayers up to God" whom she believed was "up there, somewhere."

When Jules was seventeen, she was in a major automobile accident. She was badly injured and for the next eighteen months she struggled physically and mentally—and also legally—to get her life back on track. She frequently experienced intense bouts of hopelessness.

She eventually went to Hawaii to live with a family member who offered to help her get back on her feet. She cried and prayed during the entire flight. She said, "I was begging and pleading for help. I certainly wasn't accustomed to praying, but I was desperate and had nowhere to turn."

When the doors of the plane were opened after she landed in Hawaii she experienced tremendous visual clarity—her vision had been clouded for so many months after her accident that she was slow in realizing what was happening. The colors of Hawaii's beauty were almost overwhelming.

Next, she had a clarity of thinking that she hadn't had since the accident.

While these changes were wonderful to Jules, they were also a bit frightening. She found herself apprehensive that the eye problems and thinking difficulties might recur. She almost didn't dare hope that she had been healed by God.

For three weeks, she spent hours on the beach in Kona wondering if God really had healed her. Finally, she began to praise God for what He had done, and she felt that God showed her she was at the start of a new season and a new spiritual journey. As she ran her fingers through the sand on the beach, she had an overpowering awareness that God truly cared for *her*.

Jules eventually came to the realization that the accident—which she had seen as a negative setback—was actually a wonderful blessing. It has brought her to the place of having a new personal relationship with Christ, and to a new level of trusting God. Her old strong-willed self-reliance and determination to do things *her* way was being replaced by a reliance upon God and a decision to seek God's way and then obey His directives. It was a major turnaround, one for which she was thankful.

Jules began to keep a journal, read her Bible with renewed desire, and to attend church regularly. All were like a soothing balm to her soul.

Jules had grown up without a father in her home and in the aftermath of her accident, the Lord began to fill that hole in her heart with Himself. She truly discovered her HEAVENLY Father, and relies on Him for all things. She said, "This has made all the difference in my life!"

My Friend Daisy

My friend Daisy was raised a Taoist. She went to temple with her grandmother. She told me that the statues there were very scary figures to her. She didn't really want to go to the temple, but her grandmother was very religious and forbade any of her grandchildren from even learning about other religions, especially Christianity.

When she was fourteen, her best friend at school invited her to her home for a time of Christian fellowship. Daisy thought it sounded like fun to visit her friend's home. Her friend's mother prepared a meal and her father preached. All of the children dressed in white. They sang hymns and one day they all went to the beach and the father baptized the children.

She said to me, "This friend's father was very strict and he was terrifying to me, also to my younger brother and my older sister, who had also started coming to the fellowship meetings. We decided to leave this little group—we already had a tyrant in our lives, my grandmother, and we didn't need another one.

"Through the years, I met various Christians but the more I got to know them, and they got to know me, the more I felt condemned by them—as a person who had no possibility of redemption. I also watched the way the Christians we met lived—they seemed to act one way in church or when talking about spiritual things, and an entirely different way when they thought no one was watching. I disliked that very much."

One day her sister called from Australia to encourage Daisy to go to church. She responded with a haughty, "Don't waste my money calling to talk to me about your God. If that is your topic, don't call." Daisy said, "I had a very hard heart about God and Christians—yet somehow, I managed to learn enough verses of the Bible to use in my critical attacks on Christians.

"I married and one day my step-daughter came home to visit. She had moved to Kauai and had become a Christian there. She said, 'Daisy, my dad is going to burn in hell. Do you want to do that, too?' I proudly responded with a firm YES. I said, 'If that's where he is going, I will be there, too.' I wanted Christians to leave me *alone*!

"Things started to change for me after I got involved in establishing a business with my husband. Our coaches and mentors in the business were *Christians*—but they were not like the Christians I had known in previous years. I watched them closely. They never bugged me about my lack of faith, nor did they judge me. I read the books they recommended, including a few that were Christian books. I attended the optional worship meetings, but I always did so very quietly so I wouldn't be noticed. Each time I went to one of the services, I learned a little more. It was not at all the message of judgment and condemnation I had heard as a child.

"When a new market in the Philippines opened up in our business and the opportunity was given to me to go, I went. During the trip I had my wallet stolen. The day before we were to leave the Philippines I began talking to God about this. I told Him that it was all right with me if the person who took my wallet kept the money—they probably needed it, but I wanted the photographs that were in the wallet. They could not be replaced. At the precise time I was praying, the phone rang and the person at the reception desk of the hotel told me that a person had called the hotel claiming to have found my wallet!

"Even more important to me, God led me into a new friendship with a God-loving woman named Sylvia. She was diagnosed with ALS but she asked me to visit her and help her with the business group that she had started. I went to her home thinking I would be there to help her—instead, she helped *me*. Sylvia was only able to communicate by typing with two pens held in her hands. But her heart was selfless. She was a very big inspiration to me!

"Sylvia told me about her involvement in a Bible study with a woman who had multiple sclerosis. They were reading and studying a book by Rick Warren (*The Purpose Driven Life*) which she encouraged me to get and to read. She also encouraged me to read the Bible.

"One of my business friends suggested I read a book titled *A More Excellent Way—Be in Health*. I tried to read the book but had difficulty understanding it. The man who wrote it was coming to a city in my area for a three-day conference and I decided to attend so I might figure out how this man helped people to become healthy. I heard a strong speech from a woman who was recovering her health from breast cancer. I wanted to know.

"A friend named Nancy invited me to go to a conference center for a seven-day teaching session titled *For My Life*. I went and it was the first time that I truly understood what it means to be a Christian. I had always thought I knew, but I didn't!

"I discovered that Jesus had come for me, The Condemned. I learned that if I made a choice to follow God and be obedient to Him, I would be choosing blessings for me, and for generations to come. What a revelation this was to me!

"I accepted Jesus as my Savior and was baptized. I was so amazed that I didn't have to be *perfect*—I simply had to choose to follow Jesus.

"My life changed from that week on. I met a woman who became my 'spiritual mother.' She has helped guide me in following Jesus.

"I went into my siblings' home and removed all of the Buddha statues there. My family suddenly became scared of me—they once had been quick to seek advice from me, but all that changed. They saw me as a threat.

"I felt torn and lost, but I chose to hang on to God. One evening, I came across some CDs by a well-known preacher. The CDs were a teaching series on God's grace. They helped me so much, and brought about a balance in me between God's commands and God's love.

"As I began to grow in my relationship with Christ, I found that I was confronted with several very serious problems. My father was diagnosed as being ill with a terminal disease. God helped me to pray with him and to lead him to Jesus. Almost immediately after that, I lost my job and my home.

"One night I awoke with a voice deep within me saying, 'I feed the swallows and I dress the flowers. I will take care of you.' I heard this message three times and I responded, 'OK. I got it!' God has been so faithful! He provided a much *better* job for me. I have no debts. He has given me a tremendous amount of peace. I am grateful!

"I see my purpose in life as helping others to find the truth that can set them free. I understand now why Christians 'bug' people to come to Christ and persist in bugging them. It is because Jesus is the only way to the salvation that reconciles a person to God! No other religion offers a living God who freely makes salvation available!"

Who Inspires *YOU*?

One of my great prayers for all who read this book is that each reader will find a wellspring of encouragement from the people who cross their path—such as friends, new acquaintances, people who are writing or speaking from afar. God wants *YOU* to be encouraged and stay encouraged. And then ... He wants to use YOU to encourage others! In the pages that follow I will be sharing ideas, techniques, and life helps that came to me as a result of daily asking God for wisdom and knowledge in building international business. He said to pray about everything. I took that seriously and applied it. I trust you will too.

9

A Heart for Others

When I talk to people who are potential business recruits or associates, I do not look at their clothing or general sense of style. I look into their eyes. The look there tells me what I need to know.

This does not mean that I have no regard as to whether a person is clean. Even very poor people can find a way to wash themselves and their clothing, and especially so if they believe they are going to be in the presence of someone they regard as "important."

Prior to my doing work on the international stage, I met very few people who had a look of raw, naked DESIRE in their eyes for a "better life" than what they were currently experiencing. Overseas, I saw this look often! It was intense.

"But what," you may say, "about the extremely impoverished or homeless people in America?" Even in those cases, a poor or homeless person often is hooked up with a variety of benevolent organizations that help with food, clothing, shelter, and healthcare. They, as well as their children, have access to a public school or library, and can usually gain access to someone in either the church world or government bureaucracy who can give them advice about building a more stable and purposeful life.

That kind of infrastructure doesn't exist in many places around the world—I daresay, *most* places around the world. People are often desperate to secure what they need for today, and perhaps tomorrow—and beyond tomorrow, there is no predicting or sure deal.

I consider it a great honor to help people who are in deep need, and at the same time, I also know that I can offer my help, but I can never promise sure outcomes. There are *always* factors that are directly related to what the *person* will do, and also some factors that are circumstantial to an entire group of people or to "people in general."

I cannot guarantee a good financial market. I cannot guarantee good health. I cannot guarantee that a person will experience no natural catastrophes. I cannot guarantee that "nothing bad" will happen to a person personally, or to her spouse or children.

What I can do is this:

- Share information and opportunity
- Be a model of honesty and integrity
- Extend hope
- Encourage the person to trust in God for His best outcomes in their life

Any person who does these four things is going to be a genuine force for good in her world!

The Great Privilege to Give Encouragement

I am thoroughly convinced that there is far too little encouragement in our world today. So many voices speak doom and gloom. So many people display negative attitudes and speak negative words. Let's bring on more encouragement!

In many cases, the greatest six words of encouragement are these: "I believe you can do it!"

Around the world, people have asked me in private counseling sessions, "Do you *really* think I can do it?"

People have also asked me about things that they may have heard that casts a negative aspersion on an innovative idea or a plan for building a business.

The truth is that people *can* do far more than they think they can do.

It is also true that some people are always going to be negative, and some people are crooks. That does not mean that *all* people are crooks. I assure people that I avoid dishonest people if it is at all possible. And I also assure them that I have made a choice in my life to be *positive* and to give a new idea the full benefit of a doubt, especially if that new concept has led repeatedly to good results!

There are some people who hear an idea and go gangbusters in pursuit of it. I encourage these people to slow down long enough to learn all he or she can about the idea before implementing it!

I have encountered people who assume that because they had seen me in a leadership, on-stage position, I was available to be the source of supplying all of their needs. These people have asked me to be the go-between on calls they were too embarrassed to make ... or to get an "iron" for them because they couldn't wait as long as the "housekeeping" person at the hotel had told them they might have to wait ... or to travel dozens of miles to present the business plan to a relative because they were too timid to go.

I had to learn to say a polite, "No, I cannot do that. I'm sure you will be able to figure it out."

There is a balance in giving encouragement.

Very often, there is also a need to discern a person's motivational level. Does the person really *want* a new life or to achieve a new goal?

Do You Want a Cookie?

In my early years of being in business, I often gave something I called my "would you like a cookie?" sketch. I pretended that I had just come from the kitchen with a tray of freshly baked cookies. I had made them according to the recipe, checking all along the way to make sure I hadn't left out any ingredients. And then, after I had placed the cookies on a nice tray, I took them in to my guests, asking each person, "Would you like a cookie?" A person might say, "no," and I'd go on to the next person. "Would you like a cookie?" That person might say, "Oh yes, and I think I'll take two of them. I'm really hungry and they look delicious." The third person might respond, "Not right now, but perhaps later."

I said to my audience, "These three responses are ones you are likely to hear often when you start to present your business opportunity. There are the people who will say no, the people who will give an eager yes, and those who are in the maybe category. The truth is, the cookies haven't changed their identity. They are just as delicious and just as well made. A person giving a presentation cannot allow herself to become discouraged because not everybody responds positively. Nothing about the business opportunity has changed. It is still just as good as it was, and as good as it will continue to be!"

It is important to stay objective and continue to be enthusiastic about presenting the opportunity you know is there.

Setting and Defining Goals

Also in my early day, I focused on developing teams of people who worked with me in a way that allowed them an opportunity to set personal goals and to practice various skills that would help them reach those goals.

I would invite those who had joined my business to attend a "leadership weekend" after they had been working in the business for a few months. Those who came to the weekend were invited to participate in a motivational-informational time, and also an entertainment time.

I would take a motivational-informational book to the weekend and ask each couple in attendance to take just one chapter of the book and then present its core message to the entire group—husband and wife were each given five minutes to summarize what they gleaned from the chapter. This gave everybody a chance to talk, and I learned a lot by observing what they said, how they said it, and whether one of the two people covering that chapter took more than their allotted time!

The entertainment time involved designing the set and then acting out a little skit or a musical number in which each person had a role. This brought out different sides to various personalities. I discovered things that I could use in helping develop each person so their business presentations were livelier or more engaging.

Down the road, when a person had built a team of fifty to one hundred people, I invited the people to a weekend and again, I had exercises for them to do. One of them was a problem-related situation with the question, "What would you do?" Many of the ideas that were presented as possible solutions were excellent ideas for those in attendance to incorporate into their business presentations or as means of generating an interest in their business.

I also did special coaching sessions for those who had reached a level in the business that would likely put them on stage in front of fairly large groups. I gave them some practice time in public speaking, and offered a gentle critique to help them be more effective and to keep their talks within a prescribed time limit. Everybody had a chance to speak, and their peers were invited to give suggestions about how effective each speaker had been.

Once people reached a financial level that most people in the business considered to be "successful," I met with each person to discuss their goals in life, including the legacy they wanted to leave to the world. I encouraged them to identify and begin to develop some type of "outreach" that would make the world a better place. One of my leaders started a small orphanage, another sponsored some people doing an innovative agricultural project, another person began to help widows develop a sewing business. I said to these leaders, "Find something that engages your heart. Begin to build something that you personally cannot complete in your lifetime. Have a goal that will outlive you, and that requires that you inspire others. That will be a true legacy!"

Business is a wonderful means of changing the world for the *better*. Creating a "better world" gives real meaning to a person's life, and purpose for each person's business endeavors.

Developing Teams and Their Leaders. I am not a micro-manager. I can help guide a team leader, but I am only one person with one day at a time in terms of hours to spend in helping others. I must rely on team leaders to help their team members. And I rejoice any time I see this happening ... and let me be quick to assure you, it *is* happening in places around the world.

What I know with certainty is that there are products that *can* be sold that aren't even being manufactured ... *yet*.

There are services that can be rendered for a fair fee ... but they aren't being offered *yet*.

There are businesses that can be started with a good line of income that haven't been put together ... *yet*.

Before these businesses, products, or services can be put together in ways that will reach future customers and consumers, *somebody* needs to *believe* it is possible. They need to begin to dream the dream of a better life and to dream it in a way that is realistic, motivating, and pretty much all-consuming. They need to be *hungry* for a better life, and believe it is possible to have a better life. And then, they need to be willing to put out the effort to pursue the dream in their heart.

Show me a person who is looking for a better life, and who is willing to give their time and energy toward the pursuit of that better life, and I'll show you the very person that *I* am looking for! That is *precisely* the person I can help.

I am not looking for a person who is wanting a free handout for doing nothing.

I am not looking for somebody who is expecting *another person* to take responsibility for their life, including their provision, protection, or satisfaction.

I am not looking for somebody who would rather whine about what is missing rather than pursue what is available … a person who would rather complain about what is lacking rather than evaluate the resources that are in their hand (including skills, talents, ideas) … a person who says, "Here's what you need to do for me" rather than ask, "What is it that I can do to help you?"

Regardless of the nation I am in, and regardless of the poverty a person may find as their current circumstance in life, I find that there are *some* people who believe that it is possible for them to experience a life that is more prosperous and more free (emotionally, spiritually, and in terms of opportunity) than what they currently know. They long for that new quality of life, and they are just waiting for someone to say, "Here is an opportunity for you to consider."

When given an opportunity … they clamor to know more and to sign on.

A person once said, "Life is like a carousel for most people. They are riding around in circles on artificial horses that may bob up and down, or stay stationary. They have no control about when the carrousel starts or stops. But then … someone sees a brass ring close to the outside row of horses. The person makes a move to get on an outside horse, and with every circle, reaches for that brass ring because he or she *knows* that it holds the potential for a reward.

"In my business, I am always looking for people who aren't just riding the ride of life, but who are looking for an enhanced reward in life. They are willing to shift their perspective and to reach out for the brass ring. And if they don't catch hold of it the first round, they'll try again … and again. It is that person who succeeds. And the success they enjoy is more than financial. It is a success that involves their own inner development."

Repeatedly, I find that people who are in *pursuit of a dream*—again, regardless of their culture or nation—are people who:

- Begin to turn outward toward others rather than look inward
- Begin to experience more frequent moments of joy and renewed energy, rather than feel depleted, exhausted, and depressed
- Begin to discover new ways of motivating themselves and others, rather than give sway to constant criticism or negativity

Dreams are powerful. They change people, from the inside out. And they motivate us as human beings to do far more than we have ever thought or imagined.

Find Ways to Touch the Heart!

Encouragement always works best if it is done within the context of a *relationship*.

Setting goals and building teams and establishing a network is all about *relationships*.

A genuine spiritual journey is not about religion—it is about a *relationship* with God.

And there are many creative ways to touch the heart of another person in a loving, faith-filled, dream-inspiring, positive way!

In opening other nations to various business opportunities, I usually began with people I met in the United States who had family or friends in a foreign nation. The person here in America saw great potential for his or her family to prosper, and very often made contact with their family members and friends overseas. If that person could put together a group of people interested in hearing what I had to offer, I then did my part in getting to that nation and giving my best to help start a line of business there. And ... I did my best to follow up, not only with the family and friends in America, but with those who attended the meetings overseas if the technology was available to stay in touch by means of the Internet or Skype. It was all about encouragement, and relationship.

Relationship Is Vital for Trust. There are many people in other nations who are anti-America ... but I have also discovered that within these nations, there are also many people who are pro-Americans. BUT, they will only enter into a business relationship with an American whom they come to believe is trustworthy.

In many of the places I have gone, I have taken a step beyond large-scale presentations of the business I represented. I have met with individuals and couples—who have questions or needs, and who desire personal consultation with me. Sometimes I have had as many as fifteen of these meetings in a day—before or after, or both before *and* after, a major speaking event.

Develop Your Unique Communication Style. Over time, you will find it both enjoyable and meaningful to develop your unique communication style in extending encouragement and building relationships.

For a number of years, as part of my business presentations to large audiences, I had a grand piano positioned on stage and I played, somewhat Victor Borge style, stopping part way through a selection to tell a business-related joke. I found it very effective to open my presentations with comedy, and then move to the serious challenges and practical information. I'd make pithy statements such as, "The rooster may crow, but the hen delivers the goods." Such a statement, then, could be elaborated later to emphasize the importance of having women involved in all business decisions related to a family.

Throughout the world I found that English was becoming the universal language. The whole world seems to be learning English. I want my business teams to know that I am grateful they are learning English, but I also have respect for *their* language. I just don't have the time to learn all the languages I would need to know to do business in more than thirty nations.

I always made an effort to give these pithy statements in the language of the audience members. As a person who had sung German music, and had sung in international choirs, I was very familiar with the process of learning language "phonetically" using the International Phonetic Alphabet. I had an ability to sound like a native speaker—for at least the few lines interspersed with rousing music! I could say "the rooster may crow, but the hen delivers the goods" in Hungarian ... or Turkish ... or Portuguese ....

This was a way of identifying with the audience members, who seemed always to appreciate the fact that someone had taken the time and effort to speak *their* language.

I also attempted to include local customs or traditions into my presentations when they were appropriate. Again, it was a matter of building rapport and trust.

And, of course, Borge never finished any piece of music that he started. There was a message in that, too. You never can "max" out your potential in any area of life, and you can never "max" out your potential in business. There's always a group of potential customers who have not been reached, and also a group of potential recruits and business associates that you have not contacted!

One of my favorite statements embedded in the musical performance was this:

When a woman is 20, she needs good looks.

When she is 30, she needs a good man.

When she is 40, she needs a good brain.

But when she is 50, she just needs *cash*.

Regardless of the nation, that statement was a huge hit. It apparently is a situation that knows no cultural or national boundaries!

I used this statement, of course, to reinforce the idea that when a person begins a new business, that person will need to learn a new "vocabulary" that is pertinent to the specific business. The establishment of a new business is always a learning process—not only of new terminology but new procedures and a new way of thinking. And, in truth, women of all ages and situations can always use more *cash*.

I enjoyed using humor in my presentations, but humor is different from culture to culture and it is difficult to translate. The best humorous examples were always little stories that had a funny side to them— usually stories about my own foibles, flaws, or failures. It was very difficult to find "life examples" or "word pictures" that were meaningful across all the cultures represented in a room.

For several years, I was conscious of something that may or may not have been an important factor in doing business-related presentations and motivational talks. I tried to separate the secular and the spiritual. I didn't want to offend anybody. I wanted to appeal to the greatest number of people, and to do that, I believed I needed to strip anything that might have a spiritual connotation or example from my talks.

I discovered over time that even though the business opportunities I presented were neutral in facts and concepts, the *people* in any audience were not just rational beings with no soul. There is a spiritual dimension to every person, and very basic core values have good appeal across most cultures. A focus on values is a good bridge between the secular and spiritual.

In a number of venues, I worked with interpreters I had never met before. In some cases, there were as many as ten interpreters sitting in booths in the audience interpreting a message through headsets to people who spoke the particular language represented in the crowd. I had to focus ALL of my concentration on the audience in front of me. I knew through my *ears* if the interpreter was finished interpreting so I could continue my speaking. But I knew through my *eyes* if I was connecting with the people.

It is very difficult to stay intent on looking at an audience during those moments when you are not speaking and an interpreter *is* speaking. It is a skill that I practiced until I conquered it. I discovered that there is a message that is sent from MY eyes and MY facial expressions and MY body posture that is very valuable and that can reinforce my words—but only if I continue to communicate during the moments between phrases or sentences in which I am not speaking.

That was the only way that I could stay "in the flow" of my presentation and maintain continuity of meaning. It was the only way, too, for me to stay engaged with the audience and to maintain the energy of a presentation.

In a number of cases, I would find myself flipping over some of my intended remarks so that at the end of a presentation, I truly did not know fully what I had said and what I had left unsaid.

Communication heart-to-heart is far more important than getting through a speech text or a memorized presentation. CONNECTION is what matters!

There are times when you must realize that you are facing an audience that has built-in resistance and skepticism about any new ideas on business or life in general.

In those times *especially*, you must ask the Lord to show you very clearly when to speak and when to be silent, and if you are to speak, to show you precisely what you are to say—and to give you the courage to say that and not one word more.

It is hard to do this if you are being accused of things that you know are false, or if you can see clearly the hand of evil behind what is being said against you. It is vital nonetheless that you trust the Lord completely for every minute of such an experience.

Choose Your Audiences. As much as possible, choose the audiences to whom you speak. This is not always possible if you find yourself in a small group or a one-on-one counseling session. But if you are invited to speak to a group of more than twenty people, make sure you only accept such an invitation if you believe you can truly connect with that group.

I admit that I have found it difficult to "warm up" to some cultures. If I discover early in my travel to a nation that I don't like a particular culture's music, art, cuisine, or lifestyle, then I don't choose to go there repeatedly unless the Lord speaks directly to my spirit that I am *supposed* to go. There are too many areas of the world in which I feel loved, a sympathetic or kindred spirit with their art and music, and feel safe and protected! I'd rather do business in areas where I have a good opportunity to help people who *want* my help and who welcome me with open arms. There are some nations to which travel is very difficult—long miles, bad connections, and very few amenities along the way to make the experience enjoyable.

Engineer Your Audience. Beyond choosing an audience, I recommend that you "engineer" your audience. Let me explain!

As I held early sales-related meetings, I came to a realization that I needed to invite people who were already part of my business, as well as people who were just hearing about the business for the first time. Ideally, I needed to have sixty percent of the people in the room already "on board" and enthusiastic about being in business, with only forty percent of the people "newcomers" who were interested but not yet committed. It never worked well to have an entire room filled with people who knew nothing about the business.

If someone recommended I have a one-on-one meeting with the "best person" that colleague thought might excel as a new business associate, I arranged to meet that person in an environment that was considered fairly neutral and in a relaxed way that could allow for questions and answers. I found it very *unproductive* to meet with people on turf that wasn't neutral, and that had a limited time frame. There were too many other unseen factors at work in compressed time allotments and non-neutral locations.

I never expected *everybody* in a room to respond favorably to my presentation. I looked intently into the eyes of the people in the room, and I usually could pick out those who were truly interested, and who would be persistent in working the business plan.

I always looked for family photos on display in a person's living room, or asked if a person had a photo of their children in their wallet. I wanted the person to know that I truly did *care* about the totality of their life, not just their ability to be a productive business associate. Most people are more interested in who you are and what you believe if they sense a genuine care and concern for their *children*.

Trust God with the Outcome. No matter how good you are as a communicator ... no matter how much you tailor a message to inspire or encourage others ... no matter how pure your heart may be toward establishing a relationship ... you can never be *assured* of communication success. I have become convinced that we do the communicating, but it is God who makes the CONNECTIONS.

I often have not been fully aware of what I have said, or the impact it may have had on an audience ... at the time of my speaking or shortly thereafter. In many cases, a musician or speaker is on a stage with such intense lighting that she cannot see beyond the first few rows of the audience. There is a "feeling" to a room that can generally be discerned as positive or negative, but there is little ability to look individuals in the eye and see if a message or the delivery of a song is really having the impact the performer desires. In many cases, I have had to rely upon close associates, and perhaps from responses received through the mail many months later, to indicate which of my presentations were the most effective.

I had to remind myself frequently that even if I received "good reviews"—perhaps even "rave" reviews—I should not give great importance to these compliments. Comments on another person's performance are always subjective, and it is always in the eyes of the person making the comment. I had to learn to evaluate *before the Lord* whether I had done a good job. I developed a sense of knowing whether the *Lord* was pleased with what I had said or done. And I learned that if I sensed *His* pleasure, that was the greatest pleasure I could ever know.

I began to speak and to sing and to play for the Lord as the Number One person in my audience. If He smiled, then I could rejoice.

I am sharing these things with you here because these are all very good things to keep in mind if you are seeking to share your faith with an audience, large or small. It is good to have plenty of "believers" in the room—people who know that a relationship with Christ Jesus is the best thing that has ever happened to them, now and for all eternity. It is good to meet at times with individual people to share the story about your relationship with the Lord—and to do so on neutral turf and in a relaxed time frame that allows for plenty of question-and-answer interaction.

The eyes truly are the window to the soul. And you must always seek good eye contact with another person. You'll learn so much—their level of fear or discouragement, their eagerness or reluctance, their joy or their pain ... it is all in the eyes.

10

Accomplish Something So You
Can Give Something

I strongly believe that every Christian should be a generous giver and a diligent worker. The Bible has a number of passages that relate to the value of work and call people to do their best and be as diligent in work as possible. The Bible also has numerous passages that point to God's desire that His people be great "givers." The Lord Himself is our role model. The most famous verse in all the Bible says:

"For God so loved the world that He gave ..." (John 3:16)

Jesus linked love and giving. And Jesus gave His *all*—His life was poured out on the cross on which He died. While we may not be called upon to die for our faith, we are called to live in a way that pours out all of our time, energy, and resources in faith as acts of lovingkindness.

True Integrity Never Demands "Entitlement"

Integrity does not accommodate the concept of "entitlement"—a belief that others "owe" you something solely because you have what they want and don't have.

One of the things that "bugs" me the most is the prevailing sense of "entitlement" in our world today. People expect a vast amount of something for nothing. They expect others to do for them, provide for them, and guarantee that provision and service *regardless* of what they themselves do, or are capable of doing.

When I was teaching in high school years ago, I asked one of my students one day, "What are you going to do when you graduate?" He was a senior and I fully expected him to answer me with a game plan for his coming year. He said, "I'll probably go on welfare like my mother."

I replied, "You are telling me that you have been through twelve years of schooling—and you are an intelligent person, in my opinion—and all you aspire to is to draw a welfare check?"

He shrugged and looked at me as if to say, "Why not?" It was the easiest path to a steady income he could imagine. Never mind that the income was going to be far less than what he might *earn*. Never mind that he was capable of doing a job and earning money. He had no clue that the money in the welfare system was earned by *somebody*—the "government" wasn't just a big vault that self-manufactured welfare checks.

I was dismayed—for him, for myself, for all of us.

Another time, I received a letter from a mother, and enclosed with it was a letter from her child. She stated that she didn't have *time* to earn the money her child needed. If she didn't receive $500 within a week, her daughter was going to have to quit … wait for the drum roll … *roller skating lessons.*

I was amazed. And a little appalled. And dismayed.

On yet another occasion, a man asked me for a donation to help a particular project overseas. I thought about the program in which he was involved and replied, "I'm sorry. I just don't feel led to do this right now."

He replied with a grin, "Well, you can't blame me for asking. You're usually an easy touch."

I don't mind telling you that my feelings were hurt in that moment. I like to give, and I like to feel generous and outgoing toward the needy. I do *not*, however, like to be classified as an easy touch.

Once again I was amazed … appalled … and dismayed.

Through the years I have found myself facing a similar mind-set in giving business presentations. I would walk through a proven program that had a high degree of reliability in generating income for any person willing to do the steps required … speaking as clearly and patiently as I knew how … and often there would be a person who would ask me at the end of the evening, "Will you give me a scholarship for my child to attend school?"

I had just explained how that person could earn enough money to send her own child to the school of her choice—and still, she wanted *me* to do for her what she was capable of doing herself.

Let me make my position very clear:

- I have no desire to receive a reward for doing "nothing." I have no desire to give rewards to those who do "nothing" to earn them.
- I have little regard for people who refuse to see the real effort required to attain anything of *value* in life.
- I routinely tell potential recruits, "I will work *with* you." I never offer that I will do something *for* another person. I let it be known, "If you will do your part, I will be there to do my part."

As the result of the above-mentioned experiences and many others, I finally came to the point when I said to people who asked me for a special financial gift or opportunity, "I can help you, but the best thing I can do for you right now is to tell you to listen to this CD, read that book, and then call me five days from now at ten o'clock in the morning." If the person doesn't call, I know the person doesn't want to work—he or she only wants a free handout.

All Work Is Honorable
if the Work Produces GOOD

A number of young people have told me that they cannot find a job, but when I probe further, I discover that they know of jobs that are available but they don't *want* them. They think the jobs are "below their station" in life, or that they are inadequate because they "aren't in the person's *field*." Some don't want to work for less than they think they *deserve.*

In all my years of building businesses with people around the world, I have concluded that only about ten percent of the potential recruits in my business are truly willing to put out the consistent, diligent *effort* to reach the goals they set for themselves. It isn't a matter of goals being set too high. It is a matter of people not wanting to put out the *effort*—the time, the energy, the "work"—to pursue the goals.

I have found that women on the international scene are already working hard. Many women are clearing rocks to help out at construction sites!

When I showed up and taught women that they could sell little packets of soy protein powder to their neighbors and make as much money as carrying heavy rocks on their head, they were *delighted*. The soy powder was in keeping with their vegetarian diet, it cost less than other forms of protein available to them, it made their children healthier, and it wasn't back-breaking!

A good work ethic is foundational to a person taking responsibility for her own life. When a person works and earns, and then takes responsibility for spending that money in a wise way—something wonderful happens in that woman's soul … she has increased self-esteem and self-value, she holds her head higher, and her children tend to hold her in higher esteem.

How does a parent instill such a work ethic in her children? I believe a work ethic develops when children are required by their parents to do certain chores and have responsibilities solely because they are members of a family—being a family member is a *privilege*. The same for going to school, and studying and learning and getting good grades. If all work has a dollar-amount attached to it, including the work of "study" at school, then a child begins to believe that all effort should be rewarded in tangible ways. An incentive to work for the sheer joy of accomplishing a task is often lost.

On the other hand, all work does produce rewards—many of them are intangible.

Something for SOMETHING. One of the first pieces of advice I have shared around the world is basically this: You don't get something from nothing. Even in a business that requires very low "buy in," there's a cost to pay.

I tell people, "You will need a little bit of money to get started, and you can earn that money. Don't borrow it. Don't take out a loan for it. Don't expect somebody to give it to you."

"But how?" people ask.

My reply: "There's nearly always something you have that you can sell—either in possessions or services."

- Consider having a garage sale or putting something you own and don't use out for sale in somebody else's garage sale.
- Take on a part-time job.
- Trade in your high-maintenance, high monthly payment car for a low-maintenance, low-payment car (or take public transportation).
- Provide a service you know how to provide to someone who wants that service—it may be mowing lawns, cleaning houses, giving lessons in an area of your expertise, or providing babysitting for adults, children, or pets on Saturdays.
- Consider doing some seasonal work—such as helping a person decorate their home for the holidays, house sitting for people going on vacation, or providing transportation services for someone who is housebound. If you are inclined to gardening you may want to sell produce to your neighbors, or preserve food or make jams or jellies to sell.

Also, find inexpensive ways to meet your family's daily needs. When I first moved to Oregon, I picked strawberries, beans, and pears in order to can these items to supplement our family food pantry.

Then, once you begin your business, budget yourself carefully so that you can "buy products to sell" from what you are earning. Don't overextend yourself. Make sure you keep in mind the expenses that are going to be related to your going to motivational meetings and also going to your own sales presentations. Keep things in balance.

There are two great advantages to doing these things:

First, you'll have satisfaction in paying for your own start-up fees related to your own business.

Second, you'll find "proof" that if you can spend these beyond-your-day-job hours for money-making, you'll be able to do presentations related to your new business in the same reliable and productive way!

Stay Focused on *Precisely* What You Desire to Change in Your Life. Through the years I have asked countless people, "What is it that you want to change in your life?" And, "How badly do you want that change?" It helps tremendously to get a person to focus on one tangible, focused thing that they want to see changed—it might be a new carpet on the living room floor or a more reliable washing machine. Most people have a set of things that they would love to see "fixed" or "updated" or "replaced." These things may not cost all that much—but they cost more than what the person has! It is only when a person is eager to make a change, and they begin to believe that they *can* make a change, that they will be willing to take a reasonable risk to try something new in their life.

Once you have focused on what *precisely* you desire to change in your life, ask, "Are there new skills I need to acquire to be able to do what I desire to do and achieve what I want to achieve?" My mother was a good saleswoman. She sold cookware to department store clerks, then sterling silver, and in the latter years of her life, she sold real estate. She made countless cold calls and never became discouraged.

I had a good role model for selling, but I didn't personally think I could do it. I had to make a conscious decision to LEARN how to do it.

When possible, find ways to adapt current skills you have to your new goals. As I began selling, I realized that I had lots of "carry-over" benefit from my teaching days:

- I knew how to do research and make a lesson plan.
- I knew how to communicate a message.
- I knew how to keep records and do assessments (from "taking attendance" to "giving exams").
- I knew how to measure results for both individual students and entire classes.

All of these were good skills that I could put to use in running my own small business.

The Link to Your Faith Journey

Now what do these very practical bits of advice have to do with inner values and beliefs?

Everything!

If you truly want to embark on a spiritual journey, you must recognize that there will be changes in your life. Some activities and associations may need to be eliminated; other disciplines will need to be added. You must be willing to embrace change.

There will be new "spiritual skills" for you to learn. Be willing to learn them.

You will want to spend time with godly friends, and with the Lord. You may need to develop new time-management skills.

And you will find yourself challenged by the Scriptures and by the Holy Spirit working in you to become a more generous and loving person. You will want to serve others, rather than have others serve you.

Certainly, being a Christian does not automatically give a person a work ethic. That is a choice that a person makes with her will. "I *will* get up and do good work today." "I *will* put in a full day's worth of effort for a day's worth of pay." "I *will* make something of myself."

But let me also assure you of this: Being a Christ-follower doesn't mean that you have any right or privilege to sit down and let others do the work of witnessing to the lost or building up the faithful. There are gifts God gives us, and they are given to us for the purpose of *using* them. There is effort we are expected to put out, and do so with a *servant's* heart.

The Bible tells us that whatever we do, we are to do it *heartily,* and to do it *as unto the Lord.* Colossians 3:23–24 says, "Whatsoever ye do, do it heartily, as to the Lord and not unto men; knowing that of the Lord ye shall receive the reward of the inheritance for ye serve the Lord Christ."

Those verses present very clear truths to me:

- One, the only opinion that counts is the Lord's opinion—all that we do, we must do for Him.
- Two, it is the Lord who arranges the rewards we will receive— regardless of what people around us might say or do.
- Three, we are to work diligently and persistently, eager to put out our best effort to attain the goals that we pursue.
- Four, we are to give all of our energy, time, effort, and talent toward doing things *as if* we are serving Christ Jesus. In my thinking, that means we give our very best for the King of Kings and Lord of Lords! We don't cut corners, cheat, or manipulate

others. We do not compromise our morals or make deals with the devil. We see ourselves completely under the protection and provision of the LORD and we regard our work as being that of a faithful, loyal, and hard-working servant.

Following Jesus also means that we become *uncompromising* when it comes to our values and commitment to obeying the Lord.

We are never asked by God to participate in sin, or to compromise on matters that are rooted in eternal truth. We are not asked to negotiate our belief in Jesus or to engage in activities that attack our integrity.

Women compromise their integrity in many ways. Some directly through prostitution. But there are others who compromise their integrity *in the eyes of their children* because they bring men into their lives who are abusive to their children, or who are abusive of her *in front of* her children. Still others compromise their integrity by engaging in work or in activities that do not bring honor to God.

On the one hand, inner purity does not come from having a job. It comes from having a relationship with Christ Jesus. But on the other hand, the work that we do must not be in conflict with the principles that Jesus taught. A woman must never sell her body or her reputation. She must not sell her SOUL! A woman can sell a wide variety of goods and services that are honorable and beneficial to others, and bring honor to the Lord in the process.

When is compromise warranted? Compromise can always be made in matters of "style."

If the man wants to paint the living room a certain color ...

Or go to a restaurant of his choice ...

Or spend part of the *discretionary* money in the family budget on something he wants ...

Or plan a family vacation to a place he has always wanted to visit ...

Those are "choices" that have nothing to do with eternity or the sovereignty of Jesus. They are a matter of personal *preference*.

Let me make this suggestion: In most cases, a woman is wise if she presents a choice of three colors that she likes for her husband to make the final choice ... or suggests two restaurants that are equally acceptable to her for a decision ... or brings home brochures about two vacation places that seem equally fun … she will find it much easier to yield to the final decision her husband makes!

These things have nothing to do with violating one's spiritual conscience or engaging in sinful behavior

A woman with strong integrity is a tremendous example to her children!

More to Give

Being a woman who is *accomplishing something*—earning something, developing strong character, displaying good values—is a woman who truly has something to *give*, and in most cases, she will develop a generosity in her spirit that will compel her to *want* to give.

Generosity is important to me. It indicates to me an orientation or mind-set that says, "People around me *matter*." Generosity is the opposite of greed. Greed says, "It is all about me and about what you can do for me." Generosity says, "I want to help *you* and do things for the better future of yourself and your family."

In 2010 an international company in which I was involved for a number of years gave me an award for generosity. It was the first such award they had ever given and I felt highly honored to receive it.

The Bible teaches a principle of tithing—of giving one tenth—to things that bring honor to the Lord. The "tithe" is the biblical standard for giving, but it is nearly always limited in churches to the giving of money or material goods that can be assigned monetary value. I strongly believe that Christians should not only tithe their income, but also their time. In raising my children, it was far more important for me to instill in them the giving of their *time*, because in giving their time, they nearly always were giving something of themselves—a talent they had, or items they had made or acquired.

When my granddaughter Skylar was a little girl, her mother—my daughter Debi—took her to a nursing home one Valentine's Day. She passed out red roses to the women living there. I was so proud of Debi. I don't know if Skylar remembers this event, but she certainly is going to hear about it throughout her life and she will know that she *gave* to people who needed just what she had to give—a sign of love and encouragement and value from the next generation! I was so pleased to see Skylar being taught this lesson about giving at such a young age.

The best way to transfer wealth from one generation to the next is for the parents who "made" the wealth to take their children to philanthropic ventures that the parents are sponsoring, and invite their children to contribute both ideas and effort. Children who grow up working alongside their parents in benevolent causes are much more likely to be good stewards of what they inherit, and to *further* the good that has been started by their family foundation or business.

Giving is a powerful witness to people who do not know Jesus as their Savior, or who are not pursuing an active spiritual journey.

Jesus challenged all who follow Him to be very active in sharing the "Good News" about Him to others. This means:

- We have the responsibility for being a model of integrity and honesty—a witness in our behavior and words about the love of God at work in our lives.
- We can trust God to bring opportunities our way to share in conversations what we know about Jesus.
- Any time an opportunity arises, we can encourage others to pursue the life God desires for every one of His beloved children. We don't have to speak negatively about anything, any person, or even any religion. We only need to express what it means to US to have a personal relationship with God through Jesus Christ, and to state that we believe *every* person can have a relationship with God through Jesus Christ if he or she wants it.
- We have the privilege of extending hope to people who often have very little hope, based upon God's promises regarding our future and our eternal home.

Few things are as wonderful to me as knowing that God has a plan for my life, and that it is a plan for my good. Few things are as awesome as knowing that God has made a way for me to live with Him forever in a paradise that is fantastic beyond my imagination. That's GOOD NEWS to a person who feels a lack of purpose or future.

What a privilege that is!

11

Business with a Mission

"Are you a missionary?" a person once asked me.

My answer is "yes." I am a financial missionary.

I am not linked to any one Christian denomination, but I am not reluctant to say that I am a Christian.

I do not preach Christ from a business platform—I am not on stage in other nations to present Christ, but to present a business plan and opportunity. At the same time, I make no apology for holding to Christian values and for insisting that very basic Christian values be implemented in the course of *doing* business. Those values include:

- Honesty (meaning what you say, saying only what you mean)
- Honesty in business transactions (paying one's bills on time and not manipulating people financially)
- Fair play (not playing favorites)
- Transparency in communication (making things as clear and accurate as possible)
- Kindness (in attitude and in deeds)
- Mercy to the needy (helping wherever and whenever possible)
- Respect for all people (rather than prejudice)
- Dependability and stability in character (these traits are at the core of reliability and integrity)
- Forgiveness (rather than resentment and bitterness)

- Generosity in giving (rather than greed, hoarding)
- Personal responsibility (never expecting something for nothing)

Can a person embody these values without being a Christian? Yes, I believe he or she can ... but only to a degree. These values are not at the core of a person who doesn't know Christ. To the person who is a genuine believer in Jesus as the Christ and who is seeking to follow Him daily, these values are almost automatic. They are part of the "new nature" that the Holy Spirit creates in a person. The Christian doesn't have to work up or work at these values—they are embedded in the character core of a true believer.

I am not naïve. Not everybody who claims to be a Christian truly believes in Jesus or is committed to following Him in a living, ongoing relationship. But I also am hopeful—there *are* Christians who *are* genuine believers who trust Jesus not only as their Savior but as their Lord. They rely on God to indwell them and to lead and guide them in all things. They will make mistakes—and may sin against God—but they have a heart to seek forgiveness from God and to remedy their mistakes and to live in a way that is pleasing to God and in keeping with His commandments.

The genuine "true" Christian will hold to these same values because God requires it.

Caring for Widows, Orphans, and Strangers. The Bible especially commands those who trust God to take special care of widows, orphans, and the "strangers" in their midst.

These three groups of people exist in every nation on the earth. Many women fall into the classification of widows even though their "husbands" are still alive. These are women who are badly abused by their husbands, in some cases abandoned by their husbands or divorced in a way that leaves them penniless and begging. The children of these women often receive no financial or emotional support from their "birth daddies." They, too, are abandoned, and in many cases, abused.

As for the "strangers"—countless wars and intertribal, intercultural conflicts exist around the world today. Most of these conflicts do not make headlines in America. The conflicts are real, nonetheless, and produce a vast number of refugees who migrate to areas where they are not really wanted, but may be temporarily tolerated. These people generally have no social standing and no family ties that can provide financial stability or a foundation of support.

What widows, orphans, and strangers all need are the things I seek to provide in whatever way I can. I can't solve the needs of *everybody*. In truth, I cannot provide *all* the needs of *anybody*. But I can *help*.

On the spiritual front, I seek to provide encouragement, prayer, a listening and caring heart, words of wisdom and understanding that God may impart to me, and hope.

On the practical front, I seek to offer a means of building a small business that can provide for the basic financial and material needs of a widow, her children, and those who are new refugees in an area. This means "work" or "effort." In most cases, it requires intense cooperation with others. It means following a prescribed protocol or "business plan." But if followed, this means it generates *income*. And many widows, orphans, and strangers find that they are in situations where they have *no* income other than from begging.

An income produces not only provision and a degree of protection, but also increased optimism, hope, and self-value. With increased self-esteem and optimism come better relationships with others. With better relationships come an increase in a customer base or an increase in the building of business teams. And the cycle goes around.

I saw extreme poverty when I was with my father in Mexico. I saw how difficult it was for a man to make the decision to leave his family and go to work in the United States, several hundred miles away. Even as a teenager, I had an innate understanding and heart to believe, "Surely, something can be done so this man can earn a good living right here in Mexico and never *have* to leave his family in order to provide for them."

That same way of thinking is still at the core of my soul when it comes to giving people business opportunities overseas. I want to see people prosper where they are—to live full and meaningful lives with sufficient money to pay for a good quality of life for themselves and their children, and in turn, to bring benefit to their neighborhoods, communities, and nations.

A couple of years ago a friend told me about a conversation she had with a high government leader who said, "People point to all kinds of 'problems' in the world, but I see only two major problems. One is a spiritual problem—people need to have their basic faith in a higher being kindled and energized. The second problem is poverty."

He went on to say, "People in many areas of the world do not have the basics of clean water, nutritious food, adequate shelter, and energy to fuel the basic infrastructure of their lives. If we can help the people build or develop these basics and eliminate the stranglehold of poverty on their lives, we will *automatically* eliminate a great deal of illiteracy, dissension, and disease. And, if we couple the elimination of poverty with a renewal of faith, we will see truly amazing things in the areas of morality and cooperation—again, with benefits related to the expansion of creativity and the reduction of disease. The spirituality increase and poverty decrease combine together in a synergistic way—with many positive spin-offs."

I see much of what I do in business falling in line with this man's general approach. I seek to offer people an opportunity for doing business, with products and services that truly can elevate them out of poverty. Some of the products have a direct impact on a lessening of disease and an increase in good nutrition, clean water, and greater energy resources.

At the same time, I seek to offer people renewed *hope*. I want them to begin to believe for a better life and to put their trust in God to *help* them achieve that life.

My First Day in India

My first day in India was almost my last day.

I got off the plane in Delhi and the smell in the area was so overpowering I didn't know how I was going to breathe. The area has the general smell of a very old locker room that has not been cleaned in decades. Lack of sanitation, shower facilities, and poor trash retrieval system combined with sweltering heat was stifling.

One of the first people I saw was a young girl who was begging at the airport. Her body, at least the parts I could see, was covered with leprous sores.

I had seen poverty in other nations, but nothing to the degree that I saw it in India.

The smell of extreme poverty is a mix of death and decay—animals and rotting foliage, disease, raw sewage, and old garbage.

My first instinct was to turn right around and reboard the plane back to America.

The Lord spoke into my spirit that evening a reminder from Scripture: "You can do all things through Christ Jesus." (See Philippians 4:13.)

I said, "Alright, Lord. I'll do my best."

I was staying in a nice hotel, but from my hotel room window, I could see a slum area and women who were carrying large rocks on their heads to a nearby construction site. I saw the women working in the slum and in construction, but in the distance, I saw dozens of men asleep by the side of the road. They were hoping for work but in the absence of work, they were asleep, apparently waiting for opportunity to awaken then.

I thought, "Dear Lord, what can one person—and specifically me, as one woman—do in the face of this extreme poverty, and this tremendous inequity that appears to exist between men and women?"

I did not hear any specific response from God to that statement but I did have a very clear impression that I was to do what I knew to do, trust God with the results, and make no excuses.

I didn't see how I could accomplish *anything*, but I knew that I had to forge ahead and fulfill my speaking obligations.

Let me hasten to add—happily so—that in the seventeen years since I first went to India on business, I have seen many positive changes. The Indian people are working hard to improve their nation.

My Challenge to My Indian Audience. I began my first major business address in India in this way:

"You may wonder why an American is here today."

I saw few faces with expressions that said, "Yes, I'm wondering."

I continued, "I am here to make lot of money."

Nobody was excited about that prospect—a rich American making more money out of India. That was not an appealing idea.

But I went on, "And I expect all of that money to stay in India."

Now the people were excited! I said, "I have a dream of helping a children's wing in a hospital in Calcutta to help the people of India."

The people were on board with everything I said from that point on!

The message here is this: Those who are generous toward the needy in any nation win the respect of those who are *not* needy. People are usually willing to work alongside people they perceive as being generous toward the poor, sick, and needy. You may not be able to give away *everything* you earn in a particular business, or market. But you can choose to give away a *portion* of what you earn, and to do so in meaningful ways.

The wing was improved at the hospital, and it is fully functional, helping especially children who are diagnosed with leukemia.

Toward the end of my stay, I went to Karuna, an orphanage near Mumbai our business group was developing. There I saw people sleeping on mats in the half-done construction for the first structure being built. I saw one little boy being held by his mother. He was probably only about two years old, but he had fallen and obviously had broken his arm. His mother was wrapping his arm to try to form a splint for the arm. I thought, "Here is something I can do." This woman was just one person, helping one child. I concluded, "I may just be one—but I can help at least one."

I said, "Let's get this little boy to a hospital. I will pay for his care." We did just that, and the little boy's arm was properly set and put in a cast.

What I began to see during my stay was that, although the poverty was intense all around me, the people still had a hope and ambition deep within. They *wanted* a better life for themselves and for their children. I concluded that I needed to do what I could—share the business opportunity I knew would benefit them—and in fairly rapid order, my business took off in India.

When I got back to the United States, one of the first projects I did for India was to have Rick Warren's book, *The Purpose Driven Life,* translated into Hindi, so it might be distributed to a gathering of 25,000 pastors.

Then I was privileged to help build part of the school and a dorm at the Karuna orphanage. Karuna has about two thousand students. I felt led to help give scholarships to some of the orphans who were "aging out" so they could go on for advanced training, and then work among people in the northern areas of India.

These "interns" have been going into areas where I have a number of business associates, and I am trusting God will lead them and guide them to the advantage of all those who are involved with me. God has

His messengers and His means … and they go far beyond anything that can be humanly engineered.

Later in that same year, I started lines of business in South Africa and Sweden, and I noted that India developed much more rapidly than either South Africa or Sweden. I could see that the "giving" of the Indians was directly related to their business success.

I learned that if a person is willing to give what he or she can give … and gives most or all of the profits to the people of that nation … and dedicates the entire venture to God … well, it is amazing what *God* can do, and *does!*

No Need to Reinvent the Wheel

In the early years of my business, I became acquainted with the work of an organization called World Vision, which promotes the sponsorship of children in needy areas of the world. I challenged those on my business teams, "Set up an account. Have an automatic withdrawal of $30 a month to change the life of a child who needs your help. You may never meet that child this side of eternity, but you can know with certainty that you are doing something valuable. Perhaps most importantly, you will be living 'beyond yourself.' If you are only in business to make money and meet your own needs and wants, you will soon tire of the effort. On the other hand, if you are earning so you can give and make a difference in the world, you will stay energized and motivated."

At a couple of the large meetings where I spoke about this program, I had people come up on the platform who had been "sponsored" by someone from our team through World Vision. What a wonderful life story they shared! One said, "I kept every letter ever sent to me by the person who sponsored me. They were like a lifeline to me." Another said, "My sponsor didn't leave me when I got older. Instead, my sponsor arranged for me to go to a Bible seminary in America, and then helped me after I returned home to teach others what I had learned."

I made a big pitch for sponsorship in Australia, where giving of this type was fairly new in many sectors of the society. I said to a group there, "All of you who sign up to sponsor a child will be invited to a private reception after this meeting." To my surprise, two hundred and fifty people showed up!

On one occasion, World Vision told me that they felt I had direct influence on the lives of more than ten thousand children who lived in some of the most impoverished areas of the world.

I checked out World Vision thoroughly before I began to work with them on international projects. I was privileged to be invited to some of their in-house training sessions, where I learned how their first-response team functions. These teams can be sent out within twenty-four hours of a natural catastrophe of virtually any kind. They do an amazing work. Their teams have ongoing relationships with hospitals and orphanages and other relief agencies around the world.

I believe it is very important for a person who seeks to "give" to help needy people through a major organization to deal only with reputable, time-proven organizations.

Good People Are Doing Good Things in Many Parts of the World! The more I have traveled and worked overseas, the more I seemed to come into contact with a wide variety of people who are producing some amazing products that truly have the potential to impact the world for *good*. Some are scientists, some are engineers, some are simply concerned individuals who have found a niche product for a niche need. I love doing *what I can* to help, and even more than direct help, attempt to influence others to help in ways that are often greater and more widespread.

As examples …

I have been privileged to help distribute protein bars to schools in Africa, many of which have orphan students. A chemist from India developed a protein bar that is tasty, has only a hundred calories, but has a full day's worth of protein for a child. Just one bar a day will give a child the nutrition necessary for good brain and physical tissue health. And these bars can be produced at a low cost, easily shipped, and withstand storage in hot areas of the world. How I wish more and more "ministries" would avail themselves of the opportunity to impact the health of future generations in underdeveloped nations through simple "giving" at the individual health level!

I also came into contact with a man who developed a solar-powered play-back recorder, called "Megavoice." I count it a high privilege to have helped distribute thousands of copies of the New Testament on Megavoice units in remote areas of the world. I sent units to Rwanda, Mexico, and several other nations. I once heard a man tell that he was amazed that a woman he knew was leading very good and effective Bible studies, in spite of the fact, he said, "She cannot read or write!" What he didn't know was that she had been given a Megavoice unit in her language! She didn't need to know how to read or write, only how to listen and repeat the truth that she had come to believe.

I met a couple who were running a low-wattage radio station in a very dangerous part of the world. They have to move frequently to keep their station from being located and shut down. They are a positive influence for democracy, for personal freedom, and for the Gospel—which are considered enemy ideas in the nation where they broadcast their programs. What a privilege to help them!

In many cases, people who have a real desire to help others are extremely excited and grateful for the opportunity to partner with me and others to do life-changing, eternity-impacting work.

Women Helping Women. I have a strong desire to challenge women to find ways in which they can help other women once they have reached a level of adequacy for the needs of their own lives.

In a number of places, individual women may not have had adequate resources to begin a business of their own, but if a small group of friends—perhaps four or five women—pooled their resources, they could begin a business. As the business grew and they made money, they usually parceled out the proceeds in a way that eventually allowed each woman in the group to begin a business, and along with that division, they tended to divide the customer base. They found a way!

Micro banking has been successful in many nations on that same principle—you and I work together in a way that helps you, and also helps me. In micro banking, the "bankers" have found that well more than ninety percent of the women who take out micro loans repay them, and in a timely manner. (That is a much higher rate of repayment than regular banking, and the repayment rate by male borrowers.)

I helped some women in India start a business of making pickles. The making of pickles doesn't require refrigeration, or electricity. It requires a covered pot, cucumbers, and water—and the end product can be packaged or sold in bulk at a market. It's a very simple business but a thriving, successful business for many women!

I helped other women start a business of sewing lace and also doing beadwork on garments. The women do outstanding work, and are paid well for the end product. For many women coming out of prison or abusive environments, the making of something "beautiful" has tremendous psychological benefit.

I helped still other women start a housecleaning business. This is a business that requires "trust," but not tremendous skill or intellect. Any woman can be taught to use quality products to clean a home!

I know of businesses where women make beautiful Christmas ornaments, fabric purses, and lovely scarves.

In an orphanage in South Africa—called Orlando in Soweto—we provided funds for the people there to build a beauty shop, a flower shop, and a laundry. People from the community could come for the services that were offered by the older children and those "aging out" of the orphanage program.

A Garden Grows in Soweto. I was amazed when I first heard about the work of a man in South Africa who got permission to parcel out the land under high-voltage electrical lines for use by the poor in Soweto (which stands for Southwest Township; it is one of the poorest and more strife-riddled areas in all of South Africa). The land was divided into parcels of six square feet for planting gardens. The man told me that a family of four could grow sufficient food on that amount of land to feed itself, and with adequate protein. Beans, a type of kale, tomatoes, and other quick-grow plants could provide an ongoing source of nutrition year-round. Now this area of land was not only under power lines, but it was on a slope down to a water source, which was an added advantage to garden-growers and at the same time, was a factor that kept the area from being desirable for the building of businesses or shops. It was a win-win site for the people of Soweto!

All it took was the ingenuity to see potential in the land area, and to put the gears into motion to secure permission to farm the land for the benefit of the poor. I love that type of thinking. There's no telling just how many projects could be done around the world to benefit the poor, if a person will only look for what might be done, and then be willing to put out the effort to do what it takes to implement the idea.

Geraniums Grow in East Africa. One of the most unique opportunities was one I discovered in Rwanda. Scientists had developed a process for extracting the oil from geraniums. This extract is used for aroma therapy in spas. The oil, packaged in very small vials, is easy to transport and a good added-value product for spa centers.

120

The scientists told women in the area that if they would work in this geranium extracting venture for five years, they could *own* the home that would be provided for them while they were working. What an opportunity!

And how privileged I felt to help sponsor several homes for these women willing to work hard and improve the future for their families.

One of the questions that God asked Moses at the burning-bush experience (told in Exodus chapters 3 and 4) was this: "What do you have in your hand?" That is a good question for every person to consider, especially when your back is against the wall and you don't think you have anything of value to invest in your business. It is also a very good question to ask when you are evaluating opportunities for ministry and "mission" around the world!

The Beauty of Music

Prior to entering the world of business, I was a professional musician and a music professor. Music has been my passion all my life, and especially choral conducting and piano performance.

I received a few scholarships when I was in college, and they were helpful but they certainly didn't pay the entire cost of a college degree in music. I was determined *not* to have any college loans when I graduated so I chose to work part-time during my college years. I worked in an office, and I also taught piano lessons privately.

By the time I was nearing the end of my master's degree, which was in conducting, I saw that the only way a person with a degree in music-performance conducting could really get ahead in life was by being a professional musician full-time, do recordings, or go on for my doctorate so I could teach music in a major university or college setting.

I was offered a position to study in a doctoral program, an offer that included a very fine opportunity to conduct a well-known college choir as part of the practical performance segment of the program. Then along came the business opportunity that became my full-time work! I didn't really want to leave *all* music behind me, but I could see no way to stay active in music and still build a national and then international business. I had a choice to make ... and I came to the point where I realized I could probably do more for *musicians* through my business than through a conductor's baton.

My eyes were opened when I began to sing in the Bach Festival, which is held every summer in Eugene, Oregon. What a marvelous experience that was—then, and still is today. I began to envision a new way of being an active contributor to the music world, and to give added meaning to my business efforts at the same time. I determined to give *scholarships* to worthy students—usually from other nations—so they might travel to the United States and attend the Bach Festival. I went to the conductor of the Bach Festival with my idea and he was enthusiastic.

I made contact with Helmuth Rilling, the conductor of the festival choir, and we found that we had a great deal in common. He was enthusiastic about my idea and over the years both he and his wife Martina became fast friends.

It took me about a year to build my business to the point that I could give several thousand dollars to sponsor an outstanding musician from eastern Europe to attend the festival in Oregon. I also gave money so the foreign students who came to Oregon could buy musical scores to take with them when they returned to their nations.

Helmuth Rilling told me a number of stories down through the years about his work with outstanding choirs in eastern Europe and Russia. The students loved the music of Bach, but they had no idea *what* they were really singing. They certainly knew the words and what the words meant individually and as sentences, but they did not know the Bible stories and passages that gave rise to the lyrics in Bach's work. Helmuth had a tremendous opportunity to present the Gospel message—long before it was acceptable to present the Gospel behind the Iron Curtain.

At Helmuth's request, I also bought a copy machine for a church in Budapest, as well as the toner and supplies to keep it working, so he could loan them Bach scores to perform while Hungary was still under Communist rule.

I was privileged to go to Europe a number of times to sing in choirs that Helmuth was conducting there. Very often I was the only American in the choir, singing alongside musicians from various eastern European nations, under the baton of a German conductor!

One evening during dinner after a concert in Prague, the waiter asked me if I knew the identity of a man at a nearby table. I said, "No, I don't recognize him. Who is he?" and the waiter replied, "He's our prime minister."

I said, "Do you think you could get his autograph for me?" He took the card I gave him to sign, and he said, "And who shall I say *you* are?"

I replied, "An American businesswoman."

Within seconds, it seemed, the prime minister, Vaclav Havel, was standing by my table asking, "And how do you like our city?"

I told him I was very impressed with Prague and he then asked me, "Why are you here?" I told him that I had just been part of the choir performing at the Rudolfinum concert hall. And, I had also opened a business there during my stay in the nation. He knew about the concert.

I then added, "And I recently had the privilege of giving a scholarship to the conductor of the Prague Symphony Orchestra so he might attend the Bach Festival in the United States—in Eugene, Oregon." The prime minister replied, "You did?" He seemed appreciative on behalf of his nation because I was an example of an American *giving* to his nation in a way that truly helped the people there economically and culturally.

I connected with Helmuth and his wife Martina in a number of cities across Europe. And over time, I became involved in giving "scholarships" to people who could come and help fill key roles in the choirs that Helmuth was conducting—usually five scholarships to augment the existing choir, three for women and two for men. Sometimes the guest vocalists were from other European nations, sometimes from America. It was a great opportunity to spread international good will.

When we were in Vienna, a reception was held and the mayor of Vienna was in attendance. Later, I sat next to the mayor and his wife at the concert. I had been in that same place decades before, but in the "free" seats made available to those who had shown up for a concert in the rain! As I sat in the box seat looking down at the stage, I couldn't help but think, "You've come a long way, girl." And of course, I knew deep within that it wasn't anything *I* had done, but rather, what the Lord had allowed and provided.

Helmuth was always very supportive of my business efforts in Europe, and also very appreciative of my support for his musical endeavors. He respected what I was trying to do to help people both culturally and economically. He once took me to a reception at which he was being honored for his work in reuniting West and East Germany. Present at the reception were leaders from across Germany, and

Helmuth was very kind and forthcoming in introducing me and telling what I was doing to assist people throughout Europe who needed additional income.

We tend to think, I believe, that Europeans are all sufficiently prosperous. That is not the case. There is a poverty segment in every European nation that pretty much "falls through the cracks" of provision, in spite of socialistic government programs. They sometimes are immigrants, sometimes the "widows and orphans" who do not have adequate resources, sometimes students who desire and are capable of doing so much but who cannot attend high-learning institutions for lack of finances. There is need *everywhere*, and there is tremendous fulfillment and satisfaction possible when a person can help meet that need, even in a small way.

I have been giving these scholarships since 1980. One of the most recent scholarship recipients was a young man from China. He came to me at the Bach Festival and thanked me for his scholarship. He said, "I have been able to get permission for Helmuth Rilling to come to China to conduct a Bach concert. This is the first time that China has opened its doors to the performance of a 'Christian concert' since Communism came to China." While many Americans may not associate Bach music as "Christian music," it most certainly is! Bach was not only a composer, but a Christian minister, and his choral works are all about Jesus and God's merciful forgiveness and love. The people in other nations sometimes do not understand what all of the words mean, but let me assure you, Helmuth explains the words to the performers, who readily spread the word. And, even if they do not understand the words, the audiences *do* feel the Spirit behind the words and know that they have been in a spiritual environment that is very pure and very powerful.

The Holy Spirit often gives people a direct intuitive understanding of God's truth, with or without literal translation of language. This seems to happen often in concerts that feature music composed by strong Christian believers.

When Helmuth went to China, the concert was sold out!

It was no accident that this young man who arranged the concert is a Christian. He was eager to share that information with me. I pray that this scholarship program can continue for many years.

I don't know what your "passion" is beyond your family, your business, and perhaps your church. I do know that you will find great joy in *giving* to extend your passion to others, and that the more you give in this way, the more the doors will open for you. Look for that to happen! And be bold in walking through those doors to new levels of giving!

12

Influence: Leading from Behind

I met my husband Arthur in 2002, but we did not marry until 2009. At that time, the Lord made it clear to me that I was to give up international business travel. He spoke in my heart, "I need you in Judea and Samaria." That was a reference to the biblical command of Jesus that His disciples would one day be His witnesses in Judea (where Jerusalem was located), Samaria, an area just north of Judea, and the uttermost bounds of the earth—in essence, every place other than Judea and Samaria. When the Lord spoke "Judea and Samaria" to me, I knew instantly that He was asking me to give up my extensive travels to the "uttermost bounds" of the world.

The Lord then showed me that there were other ways to communicate my message to other nations—through the new innovative electronic means of communication, such as Skype and the Internet, and through messages that might be available through international print or audio sources, also via the Internet.

He also brought to mind Psalm 144, which begins, "Blessed be the LORD my rock, Who trains my hands for war, and my fingers for battle." I instantly had an image of work on the computer and by telephone, including Skype communication. The work on computer, of course, includes *writing*—both for print communication and electronic books.

The Lord further allowed me to be introduced to the concept of "leading from the back." This was a revolutionary concept to me in many ways. "Leading from the back" means encouraging people that you allow to move into leadership positions, and to leadership of people who have previously been under your leadership. This was a tremendous means of transition for me. I did not have to be the person on stage, or take the primary role in putting together a business unit. I could train and encourage a more select group of leaders who would do the up-front, and out-in-front work of training and promotion.

I saw that I could write training materials for my leaders. A wise business counselor told me that I needed to give people a leadership opportunity. Otherwise, they would remain dependent upon me for all things. So I began to follow that pattern—sending training materials and outlines, and then following up with personal counseling.

The concept of "leading from the back" is not something that can happen overnight. It usually means weaning people away from dependency upon you ... taking a position of walking alongside them ... giving them more independence and allowing them to show more initiative ... and gradually moving them to a position in which you are "behind them all the way," cheerleading, and encouraging them in their efforts.

Using Influence to Confront Evil

I am a strong believer in having *influence*. We too often underrate influence. It can be very powerful in putting a stop to evil and bringing about justice. You may not think that you have any power or authority to do anything directly to stop evil or generate justice. But the United States of America is a nation that allows for freedom of speech and the power of the spoken and written word. Every person can write letters, including letters to the editor of your local newspaper. Every person can make telephone calls. Every person can get together a small group of women to go along to the offices of law-enforcement officials, city leaders, and state or national representatives in government, ideally with information and a proposal about what to do.

Find somebody in your area who is active *successfully* and with a track record in helping women—include that person or a representative from their group in your communication and your meetings with the civic and government leaders who *can* make and enforce laws that address problems besetting women.

In any area of evil in which you choose to take a stand and to speak out for justice, you *must* stay strong in prayer and develop a circle of praying friends who will pray for your safety.

On one of my travels I met a woman who said to me, "I need to introduce you to my friend Nita Belles." I agreed to meet with the woman and I read the book she was writing, *In Our Back Yard.* The book was about the sex trafficking that was occurring in Bend, Oregon, and all around the Pacific Northwest. I had no idea prior to that about the vast extent of sex trafficking, much less that it existed in such force in the city I call my "second home." I was appalled.

My daughter Debi and I then went to a meeting being held in Bend. A sheriff from Portland spoke to us, telling us about his interviews with a prominent pimp who was in prison. This man told his scheme: He pretended to be mentally retarded, in order to take advantage of a rule in the school system that the mentally challenged could stay in the school system until the age of twenty (thinking this would maximize the help they might receive from the educational system). He then would seek out cute girls in the high school—and even the middle school—who would take pity on him and befriend him. He would get them to go with him to coffee after school, and then invite them to a party.

At the party, the girls were abducted and sent to Seattle, where they were raped for two weeks, stripped of all their money, phone, and identity, and subjected to brain-washing that their families and nobody else would want to have anything to do with them after their sexual molestation. In most cases, the molesters threatened the girls with violence or death to their families if they ever tried to escape and return home, or contact their families. The girls were put on a prostitution circuit that included Seattle, Portland, Reno, and Bend. They were kept in closed buildings and vans, and pimped out primarily to people who attended conventions in those four cities, all of which are prominent cities for conventions and conferences owing to their fabulous scenery and amenities.

Shortly after this, I was invited to speak to a couple of groups in Michigan that were involved in rescuing girls from prostitution. My husband went to one of these meetings and became just as shocked as I was that sex trafficking could occur in such a major way in two cities— one in Oregon and one in Michigan—that we thought were bastions of morality.

I asked the Lord to show me *exactly* what I was to do about this. I knew that I could not go out on the streets at night and personally attempt to rescue the women who were trapped into this bondage. I did not feel at all led to start an organization or to become a prominent speaker on this topic. But I did have an abiding concern—and especially so, since I had a young granddaughter that was growing up in Bend (at that time). I knew I needed to do *something*.

The Lord showed me that I was to start a prayer chain, and to warn people about what was happening. My husband and I started the "Hope Unchained" email list to warn people about the rampant evils of sex trafficking. As part of the warning, we communicated not only with the people who signed up for the "Hope Unchained" emails, but we also attempted to influence key government and civic officials to take an active, even proactive, stance against sex trafficking.

I began in a very small way, but very quickly, I realized that this was a huge problem in *most* of the nations of the world.

When I went to speak to women's groups, I often included information to warn about sex trafficking. I told my audiences:

- Warn your young girls about this. Let them know that they are prime bait for men, and usually teenage boys, who have no regard for them and see them only as a means of earning a quick $500 for turning them over to a professional pimp who may be part of a highly organized ring of pimps.
- Do not let your daughters go to the mall by themselves. Even if they go with a group of their friends, make sure that every person in that group is forewarned and willing to be a loyal friend looking out for the best interests of the others who go shopping with them. The malls of our nation are prime places for girls to be enticed with free gifts and offers of modeling … with the next step often being an invitation to "come out to our promotional van and have a free photo shoot." Once a girl leaves the mall and climbs into such a van, there's no turning back for her.
- Write to those who govern your city, state, and who represent you in Washington, D.C., and register your concern about sex trafficking and all laws pertaining to prostitution and the distribution of pornography. The viewing of porn, and

distribution of porn are directly related to prostitution and sex trafficking.

- Encourage and support those who are actively fighting against sex trafficking. If you can have a part in rescuing just one girl, you will be doing a lot!

One day a woman who works with me in my business and who knew about my deep concern about sex trafficking told me that she had just taken a "second job" as the events coordinator for a major hotel located downtown in a major city. She said, "I know there is prostitution and pornography—and very likely sex trafficking—going on in this hotel and I want to do what I can to stop it." I called a friend who gave me the name of a leading law-enforcement official in her city, and she got in touch with him and together they developed a step-by-step plan to put a stop to the prostitution and pornography in that one hotel.

But the story didn't end there—this business associate worked with her employer to launch a training program throughout the hotel chain across the nation. The awareness and training program she helped develop has gone national—and even international since this hotel chain has many locations in other nations. We are now hearing that *other* hotel chains also are awakening to the fact that the taint of pornography and prostitution are *not* what they want linked to their hotels and the conferences often held in or close to their hotels.

A friend said to me not long ago, "This is such a sordid issue. How do you stay positive in your life?"

My husband and I confronted this same question several months after we began the "Hope Unchained" email list. We decided that every day, we would join in prayer against sex trafficking—asking God to free specific girls whose names we had been given as being in bondage to pimps, asking God to help those who were on the streets seeking to rescue these trapped women, asking God to bless those who were helping the women who came out of sex trafficking to build new, faith-based lives, and to ask God to move on the hearts of civic leaders, business owners, and government officials to stand strong and to enact strong laws against pornography, prostitution, and sex trafficking.

After our prayer time, we also write email messages to encourage or inform those who receive our "Hope Unchained" correspondence and then we say to the Lord, "This is in Your hands. We give our prayers and our efforts to You. We are trusting You as the only One who can truly move on the hearts of people. You are the KING!"

We say "amen" to our own prayers and then move on to do the other work that the Lord has put before us to do. We pray Ephesians 6:10–18 every day putting on the full armor of God.

We must never discount prayer as doing little, or nothing. Prayer is *something*. God hears and answers prayer! He responds to our faith voiced in prayer. He uses faith-filled prayer to do what only He *can* do. God's plan from the beginning was for men and women to have an active part in His ongoing creation and renewal of human lives, and to have freedom of choice and free will in *asking for* and *acting on* their relationship with Him.

I believe God regards all prayer as an act of our will to put our trust in Him. When we ask with faith for His best to be done in the lives of other people—not seeking something for our own pleasure or gain—He acts to produce His life within them! It is an amazing process that produces amazing miracles. But in many cases, we do not see those miracles solely because we do not ask God for them or expect them.

We *must* pray. It is the beginning point in all assaults against the enemy of our souls and efforts to bring about God's blessings to this earth!

We Each Must Make a Decision

Every person, and especially every Christian, must make a decision about WHAT God is asking him or her to do. We must pray ... listen to the Lord ... and obey.

We must refuse to hide our heads in the sand, or become so dismayed by evil that we run and hide from it.

There are very few women who can tell me a story about their life that will "shock me." That doesn't mean that I have become hardened to tragedy or that I no longer feel sorrow for those who have been badly abused, rejected, or injured. Rather, I have heard repeated stories that come back to the same truth: The heart of many people is evil and their intent is to *use* others, not cherish or help them.

I believe very strongly that

- Evil exists.
- Evil people *will* try to use you and manipulate you if you allow it.

- God desires for us to cherish and help others. His nature is love, and when we experience His love, mercy, and forgiveness, we begin to seek out ways to show love to others.

A decision is required!

WE must decide that we will turn away from evil.

WE must decide that we will not allow ourselves to be used by others in a way that is abusive, unkind, or manipulative.

WE must decide that we will receive God's love and accept His offer of forgiveness. We must believe and receive. Please note that God does not require us to "work" in order to receive His mercy and forgiveness. He does require us to RECEIVE His presence.

I encourage you to pray diligently—starting right now—for God's direction. Be willing to extend your INFLUENCE in whatever ways you can!

Conclusion

Standing by the Door

My purpose has not been to teach large Bible studies or to have a church-based ministry. It would have been easier, I think, to have pursued a church-based ministry of some type. I had been involved in church programs all my life. I knew how to put together choirs and special musical programs. I knew the Bible. I knew the Lord. I knew how to speak. I knew my way around "church politics" far better than business politics. The world of business, in many ways, was like a vast foreign missions field—where I didn't know the players, didn't know the protocols, didn't know the "language," didn't know what to do, how to do it, or when to do what. And yet, no doubt like many missionaries, I knew that I was being called to move "outside" the church structure and to attempt to bring people to a knowledge of Jesus, whom they did not know and about whom many knew little or nothing about.

I didn't know how to balance telling people about business opportunities and telling people about Jesus. I wasn't entirely sure that it was *possible* to find a balance between business and telling people about Jesus. That balance was only possible as the Lord led me into opportunities I did not engineer or attempt to create.

My purpose has been to be in the marketplace, standing by the door and inviting others to explore what God has for the totality of their life, and for their life in eternity.

Far more than tell people about a business opportunity, we need to do what we can—in practical ways, and in prayer—to fulfill God's spiritual purpose for our life and the lives of others we influence. Many years ago I spent considerable time and focus on discerning what the *Lord* saw as my spiritual purpose on this earth. I knew that everything else—anything I did in business or to assist various organizations, or even in the influence I might have on my own family members—the real purpose for my life was in the spiritual realm. I was a child of the King, and I was put on this earth to have fellowship with Him and do His bidding. I needed to discover just what that "bidding" might be!

During the most difficult emotional and business years of my life, I came across the poetic statement below. It was written by a minister named Sam Shoemaker, and has been used extensively in Alcoholics Anonymous and other twelve-step recovery programs. I have never been part of a twelve-step program so I am *especially* grateful that this statement came into my hands to help me see my life more clearly and to understand God's plan and purpose for *me*.

I Stand by the Door

I stand by the door.
I neither go too far in, nor stay too far out.
The door is the most important door in the world—
It is the door through which men walk when they find God.
There is no use my going way inside and staying there,
When so many are still outside and they, as much as I,
Crave to know where the door is.
And all that so many ever find
Is only the wall where the door ought to be.
They creep along the wall like blind men,
With outstretched, groping hands,
Feeling for a door, knowing there must be a door,
Yet they never find it.
So I stand by the door.

The most tremendous thing in the world
Is for men to find that door—the door to God.
The most important thing that any man can do
Is to take hold of one of those blind, groping hands
And put it on the latch—the latch that only clicks
And opens to the man's own touch.

Men die outside the door, as starving beggars die
On cold nights in cruel cities in the dead of winter.
Die for want of what is within their grasp.
They live on the other side of it—live because they have not
found it.

Nothing else matters compared to helping them find it,
And open it, and walk in, and find Him.
So I stand by the door.

Go in great saints; go all the way in—

Go way down into the cavernous cellars,
And way up into the spacious attics.
It is a vast, roomy house, this house where God is.
Go into the deepest of hidden casements,
Of withdrawal, of silence, of sainthood.
Some must inhabit those inner rooms
And know the depths and heights of God,
And call outside to the rest of us how wonderful it is.
Sometimes I take a deeper look in.
Sometimes venture in a little farther,
But my place seems closer to the opening.
So I stand by the door.

There is another reason why I stand there.
Some people get part way in and become afraid
Lest God and the zeal of His house devour them;
For God is so very great and asks all of us.
And these people feel a cosmic claustrophobia
And want to get out. "Let me out!" they cry.
And the people way inside only terrify them more.
Somebody must be by the door to tell them that they are
      spoiled.
For the old life, they have seen too much:
One taste of God and nothing but God will do any more.
Somebody must be watching for the frightened
Who seek to sneak out just where they came in,
To tell them how much better it is inside.
The people too far in do not see how near these are
To leaving—preoccupied with the wonder of it all.
Somebody must watch for those who have entered the door
But would like to run away. So for them too,
I stand by the door.

I admire the people who go way in.
But I wish they would not forget how it was
Before they got in. Then they would be able to help
The people who have not yet even found the door.
Or the people who want to run away again from God.
You can go in too deeply and stay in too long
And forget the people outside the door.
As for me, I shall take my old accustomed place,
Near enough to God to hear Him and know He is there,

But not so far from men as not to hear them,
And remember they are there too.

Where? Outside the door —
Thousands of them. Millions of them.
But—more important for me—
One of them, two of them, ten of them.
Whose hands I am intended to put on the latch.
So I shall stand by the door and wait
For those who seek it.

I had rather be a doorkeeper
So I stand by the door.

My dear friend, as you journey on your way to wholeness don't forget the healing and joy that comes with sharing your hurts, struggles, and victories along the way as I have shared mine with you. Be blessed. God loves you dearly. He will make a way.

NOW AVAILABLE!

Packed with timeless business wisdom and practical tips, this book gives both information and motivation! It tells HOW to succeed ... and also how to enjoy the challenge of being in entrepreneurial business at home and abroad.

The chapter headings below give the scope of the content. Each chapter is rich in anecdotal illustrations and how-to steps, with the personal life stories of a number of Beverly's longtime business associates included.

WARNING: You may not be able to put down this book once you begin it! In the author's words, "This book is for YOU."

Chapters include

Beverly Sallee Ophoff

A Woman's Guide to "BOOTSTRAPPING" a Business*

*BOOTSTRAPPING:
AN ENTREPRENEUR
STARTING A COMPANY
WITH VERY LITTLE CAPITAL

Now is YOUR time!

Beverly Sallee Ophoff
&
Dr. Arthur Ophoff

As long as Beverly can remember, her family went to church three times a week—Sunday morning, Sunday evening, and Wednesday night.

Beverly especially loved the music at these church services, and in particular, she admired one special pianist who played in the way she hoped to play the piano one day.

She remembers a moment one Sunday morning when she was only five years old. The sun was streaming through the windows of the church and this woman was playing the piano. Beverly prayed: "God, I love everyone in the whole world!" In later years as she met people who were difficult to love, God seemed to remind her of that declaration!

From the time Beverly was twelve years old, she played the piano in her church.

The words of the hymns and gospel songs became a part of her soul. She and her sister Barbara memorized Scripture passages every week to recite to their parents during the nightly family time of prayer and Bible reading. As a young child she accepted Jesus as her Savior. It wasn't until she was about thirty years old, however, that she learned what it meant to make Jesus the Lord of her life. In her words, "That changed everything."

Even in the rough years when she strayed at times from a total commitment to the Lord, God was faithful to protect her and call her back to Himself. She experienced firsthand God's tremendous grace. She says with humility and firm resolve: "Jesus is my King, my companion, and my Lord. I am here for His work and pleasure."

Throughout her early years of marriage and raising her two children—who are now adults with children of their own, Beverly was active in local church ministry—directing church choirs, playing the piano and organ, directing musicals, and leading women's ministries.

As she began to travel in her business, her faith-related speaking opportunities took her across the nation, and eventually, around the world. For many years, she traveled to Christian Women's Club meetings in the Northwest as a guest speaker. She appeared on a number of Focus on the Family broadcasts.

Beverly has served on John Maxwell's *Injoy* council, and on the Peace Plan committee at Saddleback Church for Assisting the Poor around the world. She has been an active force in the building, equipping, and pursuit of excellence in a number of orphanages, hospitals, and schools in several nations, inspiring her colleagues and coworkers to join her in generous charitable giving.

At present she is using her influence in business, government, and ministry circles to fight sex trafficking and human slavery.

Beverly maintains an active speaking schedule, and continues to lead business teams and consult with key business leaders, in her terms "using all of the technology I can to stay in touch and communicate as personally as possible."

Beverly and her husband Dr. Arthur Ophoff maintain homes in Oregon and Michigan, dividing their year to spend as much time as possible with their children and grandchildren.

29295368R00088

Printed in Great Britain
by Amazon